WHY WE TEACH

WHY WE TEACH

PREPARING YOUNG PEOPLE
FOR A FUTURE THAT'S HERE

JOHN CORRIGAN

First published 2020 46 Tebbutt Street Leichhardt NSW 2040

Cover design by Pulp Studio

Layout by Lu Sexton

Corrigan, John.

Why We Teach

ISBN 978-0-9946044-6-0 ebk 978-0-9946044-7-7

For my father

Contents

CHAPTER ONE

Introducing the case for change

Some teachers we remember for our whole lives because of the profound, positive impact that they have had on us. Elizabeth was teaching at a Sydney high school when I spoke with her in 2001. Close to retirement, Elizabeth was always surrounded by a gaggle of students who clearly wanted to spend time with her, and she clearly enjoyed spending time with them. When the subject of discipline arose during our conversation, Elizabeth observed, "In my thirty years of teaching I have never had a discipline problem, yet in this school there are two or three teachers whose sole objective on entering the classroom is to survive to the end of the lesson.[1]"

Two questions immediately came to mind: what is Elizabeth doing that makes her so effective? And why aren't the others doing it as well?

My conversation with Elizabeth initiated a long journey of discovery.

---

1 The principal of the school subsequently confirmed that Elizabeth did indeed have no discipline problems and delivered above average student outcomes.

After several months of research, the answer to the first question emerged: teachers like Elizabeth pay full attention to their students and, no matter what their students say or do, respond with kindness and compassion.

Through focus groups with students, surveys of students and teachers, and direct observation, I found that students respond to such behaviours with a desire not to disappoint or let down their teacher and to willingly do their best work.[2]

This research and analysis begged another question: why do these behaviours matter to students? Answering this was, on the surface, straightforward: they were meeting some need such that the students wanted the experience with the teacher to continue. But what was that need? Clearly, being listened to mattered to students, but why?

Why we teach addresses this question in service of a higher goal: to provide a compelling case for "the others to do it as well" and thereby progressively improve student learning and outcomes to such an extent that the very foundations of our education systems will be transformed to better match the needs of the twenty-first century.

---

2 My colleague Andrew Mowat and I used this research to develop a cognitive coaching methodology that has been an important part of our respective practices ever since. Adults respond in the same way to these behaviours, which put them in the right frame of mind for learning and growth.

A flagging system

For many years, our education systems have been perceived to be failing to deliver to their potential – not only in Australia but in many other countries[3]. Student learning and outcomes are stagnating (or declining relative to some other countries); and student mental health issues are measurably higher than in previous generations. Much effort has gone into resolving this situation; and, while it may have slowed these trends, it had certainly not reversed them.

For years, traditional practices have been stretched and systematised: curriculum has been standardised and broadened, pedagogy has become more inventive and inclusive. The burden on teachers has continually increased; although the horse is by no means deceased, we continue to flog it.

How did we get to this situation?

The underlying driver is a change in the work that is available in advanced societies.

Societies advance by solving problems. At one end of the spectrum are simple problems: those that can be readily resolved by performing a sequential set of steps. For example, if I have a dripping water tap, I can do a google search to find any number of YouTube videos that will show me a step-by-step process to resolve the problem. I just need to follow the steps and my problem is resolved. The steps to resolve

---

3 See, for example, S Thomson, 'Aussie students are a year behind students 10 years ago in science, maths and reading', *The Conversation*, 3 Dec 2019. https://theconversation.com/aussie-students-are-a-year-behind-students-10-years-ago-in-science-maths-and-reading-127013

simple problems are sequential, can be determined in advance, and can be completed by someone without high levels of skill.

By contrast, solving complicated problems requires prior experience, knowledge and some effort. Even so, each strand of effort also happens in sequential steps. An example of a complicated problem was articulated by President John F Kennedy when he said in 1961, "I believe that this nation should commit itself to achieving the goal, before this decade is out, of landing a man on the moon and returning him safely to the Earth." Just over eight years later NASA landed the first humans on the moon (and a few days later brought them back safely to earth). The solution to a complicated problem is imaginable and a pathway to resolving it can be planned out. Yes, there will be setbacks, but no-one doubts that, with enough effort and application of knowledge, a solution will be found in a step-by-step manner.

For most of human history the work available has been algorithmic in nature – that is, sequential, step-by-step – with a great deal of it not requiring much, if any, significant knowledge or decision-making. Planting and gathering of crops, standing on a factory production line and working in a call centre are all examples. This type of work has relied on our physical strength and motor skills, low-level cognitive skills (for example following a script in a call centre), or low-level social skills (for example serving in a fast food restaurant).

Since the beginning of the Industrial Revolution and especially since the end of World War Two, more work has needed high levels of knowledge. A massive increase in the knowledge base has allowed more complicated problems to be defined and then solved. The productivity growth that led to rising standards of living in the post-war boom years continues today. Computers have massively amplified our ability to handle and share information, especially with the advent of the internet (first imagined in the 1960s), the launch of the World Wide Web in the 1990s and the phenomenal rise of the search engine in the 2000s.

Education systems have been organised since World War Two to develop most of the population for straightforward algorithmic work and an increasing minority to be capable of resolving complicated problems through applying high levels of knowledge.

Complex problems

But there are problems that are in another class altogether: complex problems, in which a complete solution – meaning a pathway to resolution – cannot be mapped out at the outset and may not be achievable at all, no matter how much effort is put in. Partial solutions may be all that is possible, and these may improve over time through repeated iterations of the search for a solution.

Climate change is a very topical example of a complex problem. We can imagine a world with a stable climate, unaffected by human action, but the pathway to get there is not obvious and the road to any type of solution (even partial) requires levels of collaboration, critical thinking and willingness to change deep-seated beliefs and behaviours that make this, under current conditions, an unsolvable problem. Another at a similar scale concerns what our societies do when fossil fuels run out. In both these cases we can imagine what a world might look like, but we cannot imagine the pathway to get there, if there is one.

Increasingly, the way we approach problems at smaller scales is to use an iterative methodology to define the problem and find a solution. An example is the concept of the Minimum Viable Product, described by Eric Ries in his book *The Lean Startup[4]*, where customer feedback is an essential part of developing a product or service. Instead of fully developing a product or service and *then* releasing it (which risks putting effort into something people don't want), a version is released before being fully defined so it can be developed gradually to solve an, as yet, undefined or poorly defined need. The Agile movement also takes an adaptive approach. It began with improving software development[5], but is now being used more widely to upgrade more general processes.

Twenty-first-century challenges

Societies advance by solving and routinising simple problems; this frees time and resources that can be used to work out how to solve and routinise more complicated problems. Eventually a point is reached where complex problems become salient and the skills required to resolve them – even partially – need to be developed.

We are now at that point, meaning that we need to develop at least a minority of young people with skills to address complex problems.

---

4 E Ries, *The lean startup*, Crown Publishing Group, New York, 2011.

5 In 2001, 17 software developers published the Manifesto for Agile Software Development, in which they said that by "uncovering better ways of developing software by doing it and helping others do it," they have come to value "individuals and interactions over processes and tools, working software over comprehensive documentation, customer collaboration over contract negotiation, and responding to change over following a plan".

As compared to algorithmic work, this type of work is heuristic in nature – characterised by the need for iterative and collaborative solutions, creativity, tolerance for ambiguity and so on, often dubbed twenty-first-century skills. The table below provides one description of the component skills as proposed by the World Economic Forum in 2015.

Foundational Literacies How students apply core skills to everyday tasks	Competencies How students approach complex challenges	Character Qualities How students approach their changing environment
1. Literacy 2. Numeracy 3. Scientific literacy 4. ICT literacy 5. Financial literacy 6. Cultural and civic literacy	7. Critical thinking /problem-solving 8. Creativity 9. Communication 10. Collaboration	11. Curiosity 12. Initiative 13. Persistence/grit 14. Adaptability 15. Leadership 16. Social and cultural awareness

Source: World Economic Forum, New Vision for Education (2015)

Twenty-first century skills as formulated and published by the World Economic Forum in 2015 in New Vision for Education. These are the skills needed for heuristic work which, of course, can also enhance the search for, and resolution of, simple and complicated problems.

Three key employment trends provide further compelling reasons to prepare students for heuristic work. Firstly, as far back as 2005, the consulting firm McKinsey & Company estimated that in the United States only 30 per cent of job growth then came from algorithmic work, while 70 per cent came from heuristic work.[6]

Secondly, since the 1990s, algorithmic work that had once been central to advanced economies has shifted gradually to being done overseas in countries with less developed economies and, therefore, less expensive

6 BC Johnson, JM Manyika & LA Yee, 'The next revolution in interactions', McKinsey Quarterly, 1 Nov 2005. https://www.mckinsey.com/business-functions/organization/our-insights/the-next-revolution-in-interactions

workforces (a process known as "offshoring"). The main areas have been in simple industrial processes (stitching jeans or sneakers, for example) and simple customer service functions (such as call centres). This has increased the amount of algorithmic work in these developing economies but decreased it in advanced economies.

The third and far more significant trend is that a large proportion of the algorithmic work that remains in advanced economies – because it needs to be done in place, or suitable workforces cannot be found offshore – can increasingly be done by machines and algorithms: robots, computers and artificial intelligence (AI).

The Programme for the International Assessment of Adult Competencies (PIAAC) assesses and analyses adult skills. Its international survey[7] "measures the key cognitive and workplace skills needed for individuals to participate in society and for economies to prosper". A 2017 OECD study[8], which used PIAAC to assess whether AI can perform literacy and numeracy skills as well as people can, concluded that:

- No education system has managed to prepare most adults to perform better than what computers are close to reproducing in numeracy and literacy.

- Adults will need other types of skills that AI cannot replicate.

What the OECD assessment does not mention is that our current education systems have been optimised to prepare the majority for

7 http://www.oecd.org/skills/piaac/

8 SW Elliott, *Computers and the Future of Skill Demand*, OECD Publishing, Paris, 2017. https://doi.org/10.1787/9789264284395-en.

algorithmic work that does not need high levels of literacy or numeracy, much less the skills that AI cannot replicate (which we can presume are a subset of twenty-first-century skills illustrated in the table above).

The missing piece in this analysis is that if schools have been optimised to prepare the majority for algorithmic work which does not require advanced numeracy and literacy skills then it is not surprising that school systems do not prepare most adults to perform at higher levels in these skills.

Horses for courses

As we know, the purpose of a schooling system is to prepare young people to participate naturally and productively in current society. The education systems devised after World War Two limited the development of students in significant ways (which are explored in the following chapters), thus producing the outcomes that we see today. None of this is sinister in any way: these education systems prepared young people to participate in the societies of their time in an effective way when most work available was algorithmic in nature. Enough people developed the skills to do advanced work – perhaps not fully heuristic work but complicated enough to require at least some of the advanced skills that are needed more broadly today.

Now, for the first time in human history, a greater proportion of work available to humans is heuristic in nature – characterised by the need for high-level literacy and numeracy skills, iterative and collaborative problem solving, creativity, tolerance for ambiguity and so on.

Humankind is beginning to engage in the most significant work that it has ever faced to resolve complex problems that are existential in nature. We need every young person to have the best possible chance to contribute to this work; that is, we need young people to develop the skills that cannot be replicated by AI and that support heuristic work.

The education system generates the outputs it was designed to create – in the case of our current system, that is, largely, young people skilled for algorithmic work. If we want a different set of outcomes – high levels of numeracy and literacy and other twenty-first-century skills – we need to do more than simply tinker with the current system, which, as we have seen, is already overstretched.

Rather than continuing to flog the flagging horse, we need to recognise that change is needed at a system level. It is time to get off the horse and into the car, which is better able to carry the load that society needs it to.

The way forward

This book aims to show what the metaphorical car looks like and how to switch vehicles along the way. It will demonstrate that system change has already begun, and that making this change explicit will get our education systems back onto a growth path, preparing young people to engage capably in a modern society that is facing existential issues such as climate change and resource depletion.

I will argue that the heart of this change is how adults in a school extend their capabilities to support a more broad-based development of students leading to greater levels of meaning and purpose, autonomy, and the acquisition of twenty-first-century skills; furthermore, that, as education is a service sector where productive activity takes place between humans, change can be relatively rapid (compared with manufacturing[9], for instance).

In chapter 2 we will look at how we grow, unpacking our three innate drives for competence, autonomy and meaning. Chapter 3 will explore how our current education systems, developed after World War Two, support and limit growth. Chapter 4 is a case study showing what is possible when some of the constraints are loosened and young people can grow without being held back, while chapter 5 will show why we need to lift the limits on growth and argue that young people are ready for this. The costs of our current system will be examined in detail in chapter 6. Chapters 7 and 8 consider how teachers' roles are changing, and how student outcomes – and the value of the teaching profession – could be increased when teachers are supported to facilitate student growth. Chapter 9 shows a student's perspective, while Chapters 10 and 11 explore the capabilities required to support students to develop autonomy and higher levels of consciousness, respectively.

The final chapter shows that there are no downsides to building these capabilities to support a broader and healthier development of our young people; indeed, that such a shift will increase the value of the teaching profession enormously to the great benefit of its members, their students and society.

---

9 Consider the effort required to switch to electric-powered vehicles: research to develop the capability for commercial vehicles; building new factories and retooling or shutting down existing factories; developing new supply chains; building mines to source higher quantities of raw materials such as lithium; and so on. Compared with change in a service sector, this is a much more difficult process that will likely stretch over decades.

CHAPTER TWO

How we grow

*"It is easier to build strong children
than to repair broken men."*

Frederick Douglass

Beginning in the 1970s Edward Deci proposed that we are driven by three innate psychological needs: to be competent; to have autonomy, and to have meaning or connection. His extensive research into intrinsic motivation led to his theory of motivation and personality known as self-determination theory[10]. The three drives, which are obvious during childhood, continue to animate our development after we are physically grown.

In this chapter, I will explore how these three innate drives are important throughout our lives and, in particular, how they contribute to our overall development of consciousness.

---

10 RM Ryan & EL Deci, *Self-determination theory: Basic psychological needs in motivation, development, and wellness,* The Guilford Press, New York, 2017. (For a more popular treatment *see* DH Pink, *Drive: The surprising truth about what motivates us,* Riverhead Books, New York, 2009.)

Our drive for competence

The most obvious need that children have is the need for competence. A young child piles bricks on each other and, when they fall, starts again, gradually becoming more competent in the use of their fine motor skills and in their judgements about placement to prevent a crash. Play is characteristic of children and reflects an innate drive towards competence – that is, the knowledge, skills and judgements that allow us to be effective in the world.

Our level of competence – whatever our age – is delimited by our abilities, which may include motor skills, cognitive ability, understanding and prior levels of competence; as well as by the level of support available from teachers, leaders or colleagues, and the opportunities available to experiment – to play. Nevertheless, the capacity to increase our competence is with us always and, when we feel good about ourselves, it is easy to follow this innate drive and become more competent still.

As we will see later in this and the following chapters, the drive for competence is linked to our drive for meaning, in that the extent of our consciousness – the way we make sense of our world – limits how competent we can become.

Schools cater to the need for competence extraordinarily well. When we talk about education being key to success in life, we mean that children acquire competence in a range of areas that allow them to be productive members of society. Every country that has developed has done so through a strong focus on education. China is a good example where its cultural revolution (1966–1976) built an education infrastructure throughout its largely illiterate hinterlands providing the workforce that has powered its remarkable industrial and general economic development since then.

Our internal need for autonomy

We all want some measure of control over how we use our time and energy. This allows us to use these resources in meaningful ways, thus elevating our sense of wellbeing and satisfaction with who we are and how we act in the world. To be autonomous, I do not necessarily need to have control over everything I do, because I always have control over how I think about what I do.

An aspect of autonomy is self-motivation: I choose to do my best without the need for anyone to supervise or push me to do so. Self-motivation can arise from an interest or enjoyment in doing the task in hand, or a desire not to disappoint or let someone down (a family member or a teacher, for example) or a desire to meet a longer-term goal or commitment (such as developing as an athlete or a musician). In each case, I am using my time and energy in a way that is meaningful for me even though the actual task may not be interesting or enjoyable in and of itself.

Historically, using controlled motivation – rewards and punishments – was thought to be the most effective way to get people to work. It was standard in schools, which made sense in an environment where most workplaces were also controlled through reward and punishment. However, this supresses autonomy and gives rise to other consequences, which are discussed in chapter 6.

The use of rewards and punishments is now changing. We know now that people are more self-motivated when they have autonomy. Indeed, as we will see, supporting students' autonomy is critical to enabling students to develop fully; it is, furthermore, a key reason why teachers like Elizabeth have no discipline issues in their classrooms.

Our drive for meaning

Holocaust survivor and psychiatrist Viktor Frankl wrote: "Man's search for meaning is the primary motivation in his life and not a 'secondary rationalization' of instinctual drives."[11]

To be healthy, functioning people, we need to feel good about ourselves. We need to feel that our time and energy is spent in meaningful ways. Meaning nourishes us. When we run out of meaning, everything else slows and stops. We get depressed.

We continue to develop and grow our capacity to make meaning throughout our lives. What was meaningful in the past may no longer hold meaning for us now; a childhood obsession over collecting sports scores or playing with Barbie dolls no longer holds meaning for us as adults. We are continually seekers of meaning. Yet, although we seek, we may not always find – for instance, if we lack the support to do so – and this can diminish our wellbeing.

We generate meaning primarily through relationships. The most meaningful tend to be relationships with other people, but we also have

---

11 VE Frankl, *Man's search for meaning*, Beacon Press, Boston, 2006.

relationships with our inner selves, our career, our community and religious, political or other groups with which we identify, as well as with ideas and activities we engage in. Any or all of these relationships can give our lives meaning and, therefore, make us feel good about ourselves.

Relationships that give our lives meaning also define our understanding of ourselves. I am a teacher because of my relationship with teaching. I am a son because of my relationship with my parents. I am an Australian because of my relationship with my country. Losing any of these things – a job, for example – will likely cause a crisis of identity because what has given my life so much meaning is no longer available.

When one of these relationships is lost, that part of our identity is lost with it. The more meaning the relationship gave and the greater its role in my identity, the more debilitating the loss. As personal relationships usually give us most meaning (and therefore nourish us most), loss of these relationships hurt most.

When we lose a relationship, the meaning it brought is stripped away and we feel a sense of emptiness where that meaning used to be. This lack of meaning – this internal emptiness – is depression. The deeper the depression, the greater the lack of meaning, to the point where a person will struggle to get up in the morning, to shower, to speak to other people, to eat, or to engage in anything really. The healthy response to loss is to gradually construct new relationships and bring new meaning into one's life.

How consciousness develops in response to our drive for meaning

As we grow, the way we relate to the world also evolves in a predictable way. We know from Jean Piaget's pioneering work in child development that children pass through a series of recognisable stages of ego or consciousness: the way children relate to the world and make sense of it changes as their consciousness develops. While it is less obvious in adulthood and less widely recognised, this development of consciousness continues throughout our lives[12].

The STAGES model of development developed by Terri O'Fallon[13] maps the development of consciousness through childhood and beyond, describing how people think, feel and behave at different stages of development.

---

12 The drive for meaning is active our whole lives but that does not mean the conditions are right for growth to occur. As we will see in chapter 6, about 60 per cent of adults do not feel good about themselves in the work that they currently do but there is not the support for them to shift to a new relationship with their work that would provide a more meaningful activity.

13 T O'Fallon, N Polissar, M Blazej Neradilek & T Murray, 'The validation of a new scoring method for assessing ego development based on three dimensions of language', Heliyon, vol. 6, no. 3, 2020. doi: 10.1016/j. heliyon.2020.e03472
See also https://www.stagesinternational.com. O'Fallon's work builds on the work of Jane Loevinger, whose development model was first proposed in 1976 but her ideas are best expressed in *Measuring ego development* (Hy and Loevinger, 1996), which includes a description of the Sentence Completion Test (SCT) used to develop it. This model was further developed by Susanne Cook-Greuter (see *Postautonomous ego development: A study of its nature and measurement, 1999*). The SCT has been a grounded data collection approach for nearly 40 years, supported by hundreds of research studies, and is a well-documented developmental approach.

The stages of development are organised into three tiers. As shown below, a newborn begins their development journey at the Impulsive stage, at the beginning of the first tier, and most young people will have reached the Conformist stage – the limit of this tier – by their teenage years.

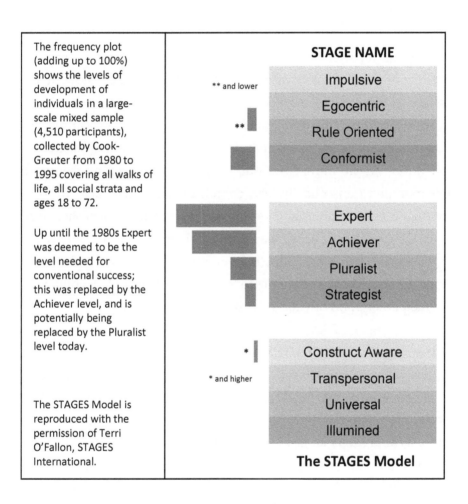

The frequency plot (adding up to 100%) shows the levels of development of individuals in a large-scale mixed sample (4,510 participants), collected by Cook-Greuter from 1980 to 1995 covering all walks of life, all social strata and ages 18 to 72.

Up until the 1980s Expert was deemed to be the level needed for conventional success; this was replaced by the Achiever level, and is potentially being replaced by the Pluralist level today.

The STAGES Model is reproduced with the permission of Terri O'Fallon, STAGES International.

STAGE NAME

Impulsive — ** and lower

Egocentric

Rule Oriented — **

Conformist

Expert

Achiever

Pluralist

Strategist

Construct Aware — *

Transpersonal — * and higher

Universal

Illumined

The STAGES Model

The current view is that we develop through our relationships – specifically, through the interplay of our relationship with our self and with the world around us: that is, the people and objects within that world.

Relationships evolve and change as a child grows. For example, at three or four years old, a child relates to the world in a very self-centred way – they prefer the toy to the friend – typical at the Egocentric level of development. At seven or eight they prefer the friend to the toy; their way of relating to the world around them has changed. This is typical behaviour in the Rule Oriented stage of development.

Each stage represents the way we make meaning from a range of experiences: information we receive through our senses; how others behave in response to our actions; and varying but increasing levels of introspection. This development of consciousness also influences how we develop capabilities that enable us to take effective action in the world. As we move from one stage to a more complex one, we integrate and transcend the less complex stage. Each stage we pass through is still within us and we can still operate from an earlier stage if that is appropriate, or we may drop involuntarily to an earlier stage, especially if tired or stressed. However, we will usually try and operate from the highest stage that we have reached. Appendix 1 contains a detailed description of each stage in the first two tiers.

A key feature of the STAGES model is the recognition that repeating patterns appear as people move through the stages in each tier; this helps to inform how people develop. Each tier represents a different content of thought: concrete in tier one; subtle in tier two; and metaware in tier three. Within each tier, however, are two levels of social consciousness – individual and collective – which reflect increasing complexity in perspective in each tier, from first-person (it's all about me), second and third-person perspectives (the latter being the basis for scientific enquiry) and fourth-person perspective (an appreciation of context). Further, four learning styles are represented in each tier (receptive, active, reciprocal, interpenetrative), each of which corresponds to a distinct stage. So, within each tier, individuals evolve through two different levels of social awareness and four different learning styles. This same evolution occurs again in the next tier, based on a different object of thought.

Transition from one stage to the next

So how does the shift from one stage to the next occur?

A shift occurs when we can no longer make sense of, or act effectively in, the world at our current stage. No-one knows exactly why this occurs or if a shift can be accelerated, although we do know we can be held back in our current stage or the shift can be extended beyond its natural term. For the individual in transition it can be very frustrating and take up a great deal of their emotional energy as they struggle to find a new equilibrium.

Change can be mediated by a destabilising event (a shock) such that the individual can no longer make meaning of the world with their existing ways of relating and they are forced to adapt and evolve their relationships.

Developmental psychologist Robert Kegan describes the process from the point of view of an adult (such as a parent or teacher) supporting a child, identifying three distinct phases[14]:

- Holding on: the child is with an adult or adults that support their current stage of development.

---

14 R Kegan, *The evolving self: Problem and process in human development*, Harvard University Press, Cambridge MA, 1982.

- Letting go: the adult or adults allow the child to push their behaviour in the world towards the next development stage, resisting the urge to hold them back.

- Remaining in place: the adult or adults welcome the child back into an environment that supports the new level of development.

The research conducted with adults indicates that, for someone to transition to the next stage, they must be emotionally invested in wanting to succeed (or they might just give up); and they need to be in an environment supportive of the change. This support may be provided by individuals, or it may be structural.

Thus, supporting a child's developmental transition from one stage of consciousness to the next can happen in two ways:

- An adult can hold the child through the process through holding on, letting go and remaining in place.

- The phases can be split such that one adult holds the first phase, a shock is provided (such as going to school; moving from primary to secondary) and a different adult holds the second phase.

In the latter situation, the first and second adults behave differently – relate differently to the child – each supporting the appropriate stage of development. As we will see in the next chapter, this is routine in most schools: teachers relate to primary-aged children in one way; and secondary children in another. However, adults do not need to think about their behaviour as supporting a particular stage of development, because all children are expected to be at the Rule Oriented stage in primary school and the Conformist stage in secondary school.

CHAPTER THREE

How schools support growth

"If we teach today's students as we taught yesterday's, we rob them of tomorrow."

John Dewey

"School is the advertising agency which makes you believe that you need the society as it is."

Ivan Illich

We saw in chapter 2 that humans, as well as developing physically, have an internal need to develop meaning through relationship with self, others and the world (our "why"); to be competent – to develop skills and knowledge to act successfully in the world (our "what"); and to be autonomous – to have a measure of control over one's thoughts and actions (our "how").

The development of these drives begins as soon as a baby enters the world. Young children begin life in the Impulsive stage of development and transition at around eighteen months to the Egocentric stage. Both these stages have a first-person perspective (it's all about me). The main activity that the young child engages in is play, which allows a child to learn about and to act in the world around them

The Impulsive stage is receptive: the baby is taking in new experiences through its senses and learning who they are as distinct from the world around them. The Egocentric stage is active: the child experiments with what they can do in the world with this body that they have. Their capacity for making meaning of the world is expanding and this expansion comes from their interaction with their environment.

We can readily observe that children have been brought up in a range of environments from the life-enhancing to the life-sapping. Immediately after World War Two, Authoritarian/Condition/Play was the dominant child-rearing approach, with corporal punishment being widespread and accepted; whereas Authoritative/Nurture/Play is now viewed as being the better environment for healthy growth.

Pre-school and early learning centres, at their best, provide authoritative, nurturing and playful environments that try to ensure that every child has the best possible start, irrespective of actual home conditions, and are seen as one of the most effective investments a society can make to avoid costly dysfunctions (crime, mental health issues, substance abuse, domestic violence) as children grow into adults and take up roles in society[15].

---

15 See, for example, a recent analysis of early years intervention in Australia https://www.thefrontproject.org.au/images/downloads/Cost-benefit%20analysis_ brochure.pdf

Supporting consciousness development

Formal schooling begins anywhere between three and seven years old depending where you are in the world; six years old probably being the most common age.

Ideally, children start school around the time they are transitioning from the Egocentric to Rule Oriented development stage, the first stage where the child can take a second-person perspective and begin to prefer the friend to the toy. Most primary school environments support Rule Oriented behaviours, (which are prevalent up to around 10 to 12 years) until the transition to secondary school. The way secondary teachers relate to students tends to support the Conformist stage, which typically emerges at around age 10 to 13. Both these stages of consciousness handle concrete objects of thought (things we can see, hear, touch, taste or smell – or imagine we can do so; emotions we can see on the outside such as sad, glad and mad).

Schools, therefore, support students' development of consciousness implicitly; the shift in the way teachers relate to students (and therefore support or limit students' consciousness development) is built into the school system itself. Children who may have been ready to shift earlier are held back in such a set up; but most, if not all, children make these shifts as the system requires. There is no requirement for teachers to think explicitly about supporting the drive for meaning and development of consciousness, and thus it is essentially invisible within the system.

A focus on competency

Our education systems were set up after World War Two to prepare most people to do algorithmic work under the direction of others, providing a simple and secure standard of living in return. It has been enormously successful at doing so and this largely remains the predominant focus of the current schooling model.

This focus created an emphasis on the "what" and a very prescriptive "how" (control through reward and punishment). Teachers were required to transfer a prescribed content – knowledge and skills – and to control their classes. Only a limited number of people had the necessary knowledge base to be able to teach – and teaching was a valued occupation. Most used controlled motivation, reflecting the dominant culture in society. Support for development of consciousness – the "why" – went no further than what was needed for algorithmic work.

Within this context of compulsory state schooling, children's development over the last seventy years has been relatively stable. Children move through predictable stages; schooling has been matched to, and in some sense creates, this rhythm: providing destabilising shocks at key moments, and necessary inputs to ensure that the transitions take place successfully, with adults on either side providing the support for the relevant stage of development.

The innate needs of children have been addressed through an overarching focus on developing competence within the limits of the consciousness development built into the schooling system; however, autonomy was curbed using controlled motivation.

Consciousness and competency

In the Rule Oriented and Conformist stages of development, which schools cater to, the content of thought is concrete: things that we can see, hear, touch, taste or smell, or imagine we can (we can see a cow, we can imagine a pink cow). Learning in this context lends itself readily to memorisation and testing of recall with levels of competence easily assessed by how well one performs such tests. Competence is built largely on memorised knowledge and the manipulation of concrete objects and thoughts, such as solving quadratic equations through a series of defined steps, themselves memorised and practised.

However, to go beyond this level of competency, young minds need to develop their capacity to make meaning so they can handle abstract thoughts and objects such as ideas, goals, abstract theories, contexts, assumptions; and subtle internal feelings such as compassion or ambiguity. These are minimum, essential capacities needed for heuristic work.

It is at the Expert stage of development that abstract thinking becomes possible; here much more complex learning – and higher levels of competence – can begin to occur. Changes in curriculum and pedagogy over the last twenty years have moved in the direction of supporting this more complex learning. Yet, to handle this complexity students' meaning making capacity must expand to the appropriate level.

The post-war education system has been enormously successful in developing people to do algorithmic work under direction. However, it has limited our children in the two key areas of developing consciousness and autonomy – and by necessity, limited the development of competence within these constraints. Young people had the skills and competences that allowed them to fit naturally and productively into the society of the time. However, this system is no longer meeting society's needs.

In a dynamic ecosystem, individual schools, individual teachers and individual school leaders most certainly developed some young people more in the direction of heuristic work due to their own beliefs about education and young people's abilities. Similarly, the harsh authoritarian nature of schooling systems immediately post-war – with corporal punishment being widely practiced – has changed considerably: corporal punishment has effectively disappeared and the physical punishment of young people in society more broadly has largely become taboo.

Things have not stood still but have moved in the direction of being more supportive of students' autonomy; and, in more isolated cases, of their consciousness development. The increase in pre-school provision is a good illustration of the move towards supporting all our innate drives in healthy ways from as early as possible.

We need this to happen on a much broader scale if schools are to develop the majority of students with twenty-first-century skills.

CHAPTER FOUR

Another way: Case study 1

A small number of schools have chosen to operate differently. The Brisbane Independent School (BIS) has organised itself to make consciousness development visible. Children are supported at their current stage of development, moving class as their development stage begins to shift.

In this chapter, we will hear from the school principal and from a former student, Jackson (not his real name) who also attended state primary and secondary schools, providing a good basis for comparison. Jackson attended BIS from grades one to seven, except for two years between grades four and six largely spent in a state primary school. He then attended a state high school to year 10 and an independent college in year 11.

BIS is an unaffiliated independent primary school established in 1968 by a group of lecturers and professionals who wanted more for their children's education than could be found in any school available in Brisbane at the time.

The school has always been a fierce proponent of progressive and experimental philosophies of education. Its core goal throughout has been providing the best education for the whole child. This has seen some successful as well as unsuccessful models implemented over its 50 years.

Since BIS began exploring Integral theory and Developmental Theory in 2011, it has become increasingly obvious that students and staff were challenging some key assumptions about age expectations around development perspectives. The school was seeing students shift into later stage awareness (Expert stage) at age 11, shifts that were once rare. To accommodate this change in expected age for shifts into the subtle tier, BIS redeveloped their curriculum to provide for these early developers. This was one of the key deciders for developing the current teaching and learning methodology.

Jennifer Haynes, Principal at Brisbane Independent School

Here, Jen explains how the school is organised around stages of consciousness development rather than by age:

It's at four-and-a-half to five that you'll see them coming in late Egocentric. Some students are early Rule Oriented at that age. So, if that's the case, they don't seem to be in Big Cats [Egocentric class] very long.

So, four-and-a-half they come in Egocentric, then they'll start to transition into the Kestrels [transition class Egocentric to Rule Oriented] usually from around five to five-and-a-half, sometimes it's six. Then they transition into the Penguins (Rule Oriented) room from six to seven and they'll stay in there until they're around eight-and-a-half to nine.

Then they go into the Otters (transition Rule Oriented to Conformist) from around eight-and-a-half to nine-and-a-half, sometimes 10. And then they'll go into the Dolphins (Conformist) from around 10-and-a-half. But I've got a couple of students that have gone over there at nine-and-a-half. And then it's the same as the transition to high school.

If they've early-transitioned into the Dolphins, academically they're ready to go to high school. We have quite a few kids who go to high school a year early, because they're so ready to shift into a solid Conformist stage; they're beginning to shift into Experts and it's torturous for them: "Oh gosh, I can't stand one more home schools meeting".

Jen goes on to talk about some of the unexpected stage developments that she has seen:

About four years ago Terri O'Fallon did assessments of our kids. There were three kids that year, two kids in the Dolphins room who were already moving into Expert, according to her assessment, and one student who was in the Penguins room: he was eight and he was moving into Expert. He became a little bit of an experiment for us, with his parents, and we went, "Okay, well, if he's moving into expert, let's teach him that way." Which has been very interesting because social and emotional-wise, he was ready for the type of collective awareness that would have been happening for Experts, but he wasn't physically ready. When they go places, he had learned that, to get information that he needed out of adults, he couldn't talk to them as equals, he had to be cute. So that was his default. He'd be cute. And it was only when we started to say, "You know that thing you are doing, you don't need to do that. Just ask me." And then he'd literally just drop it. And he'd go, "Oh, all right, well what I'm after is ..." And he'd just be a person instead of doing this strange, cute kid thing, but he'd found that that was the only way that he could get stuff organised that he needed to get organised.

Jackson, former student at Brisbane Independent School

Here is Jackson's take on his experience at BIS:

It was very different learning at BIS than it was learning in a standard state school environment. I learned a lot more valuable skills from BIS than I learned from other schools. The drive at BIS is to teach kids how to be humans. They treat kids like humans, which is a surprisingly rare occurrence, and it's very helpful. They understand that kids are hyperactive. They like to do stuff. They want to learn, just not in the way that a lot of it is really structured. Of course, the standard teacher standing in front of the class, that works for some kids, but for some kids it doesn't, and BIS really understands that. It teaches kids to understand the best way that they learn, so that they can apply that in their education endeavours, which was really important when I stepped into the state schools, because I really struggled with the way those lessons and all of that stuff was structured. But BIS had given me the foundational knowledge of self-reflection on how I would best deal with information, and the freedom that BIS gave me to explore the things that I was interested in, as opposed to more rigorous, standardised work was probably the most important thing to lead me to the person that I am today.

Teachers at BIS compared with the state primary school

Again, it falls back to the treating kids like human beings, where teachers are still an authority figure. They're still a teacher, but there's more of, not an even playing field, but it's more of a relationship where you're providing the kids with information and they're trying to learn from you and you treat each other with respect because you respect each other. Whereas I feel in state schools, it comes down to the things like you have to ask to go to the bathroom at a state school, which is one of the most demeaning things. That's not something that's going to happen in the rest of your adult life. You're not going to have to sit in an office job and put up your hand and ask your manager if you could use the restroom. It's a very strange power dynamic, that is not very productive to be learning. Even if you have a good teacher, a really nice teacher, that dynamic is still there. It's built into the institution, and BIS really lowers that wall where you understand that the teacher is in control, because they're the adult and they're the teacher, but you also understand that it's not a controlling thing. You can still go to the bathroom without asking permission. That sort of stuff.

Moving to high school

There was a series of circumstances that caused me to miss six to eight months of school and I wasn't able to get my QCE [Queensland Certificate of Education]. The faster option was to completely drop out of high school and take a tertiary admission test and go straight to university instead of finishing high school, so instead of going into grade 12, I went straight into university.

The transition to secondary school was interesting, because I only spent probably a year and a half at a state school in my primary education. I was already familiar with the systems, but it was a very odd transition. BIS geared me very well for the social aspects, because of the way BIS is and the way it teaches you to be. At least in my experience, I was very comfortable with who I was. I was pretty okay with being weird. I was fine with who I was as a person, and I feel like a lot of the early parts of high school, most of high school, for a lot of people is a lot of insecurity and trying to figure out who you are. I feel BIS had laid the groundwork for that to already be done, so when I entered high school, I was pretty socially confident.

It felt like I was in a different spot than a lot of other people were. BIS tends to focus more on other developmental things outside of just schoolwork, where a lot of state schools don't. Everyone was on the same level in their academic journey when everyone was entering high school, but I feel like I had, not that I'd developed more social skills, but I was more aware of who I was as a person and all of that sort of stuff entering it. And it was very weird.

I'm already a pretty socially anxious and awkward person, and it made that a little bit weirder because I was perfectly fine with talking about things that I was interested in and liking music that's "for girls". That sort of stuff. People go through this thing where you can't like anything in high school. It has to be ironic liking. In high school, you can't genuinely be passionate for anything, because that's showing emotion and that's weird. I'd already ascended past that. I was just like, "I don't care. I really enjoy things. I'm allowed to really enjoy things. You're allowed to really enjoy things. You don't have to be weird about it. You don't have to pretend you don't." That was the most weird thing in social interactions, because you'd be talking about stuff and people would be pretending not to like stuff and you'd know that they were pretending because they felt uncomfortable with other people knowing that they liked things. It made a very weird social dynamic where it was bizarre.

I think I regressed and then went back, because I entered high school at that [Expert level] and then the pressure of social stuff, I regressed back into that, "No, I don't like having fun" just like everyone else. And then when I was around 16 or 17, I went back to you know what, screw that. I'm just going back to be like, I'm okay with being weird again. It's fine.

As I mentioned, BIS leans into kids being kids and kids being humans and wanting to learn. There are so many things to learn and things to do. In high school when they're like, "No, you need to pick. You need to do maths. You need to do this. You need to pick the thing that you're going to do." And I'm like, "Well, I want to do everything, though." And that was probably the biggest, most striking thing to me was how limiting it was to not be able to do things. Not only do things that I wanted to do, but also not do things at my own pace and in my own way, because BIS does still meet all the testing standards. They still do tests and examinations. Kids are still graded and all of that, but the teachers and then the school understands that kids are going to be at different levels. Having a standard for anything is going to be difficult and ultimately detrimental.

Not being able to take things at my own pace and not having a school that understands that I do things differently or need different things in high school, because as well as being a secondary school, it was also a much larger school with over a thousand students. They can't really put in the same sort of things that BIS has in place with the smaller student size. The transition wasn't difficult, it was just very jarring. I could adapt, but it was weird because again, going from being generally treated well to being a student in a classroom where the teachers all mildly hate their jobs and are angry at kids for existing and all of that sort of stuff, it was very odd.

[The teachers that stood out] seem to have a genuine passion for the things that they taught. On top of being good teachers and being pleasant to be around, they really, really enjoyed teaching and the subjects that they taught, and it showed. I can't speak for all teachers, but I'm sure you have to have, at some point, really enjoyed the thing that you are teaching in order to be teaching it. You have to sit through years of school and then placements, and then get an actual position. A lot of the education system seems to grind down teachers as much as it grinds down students. And these teachers that I really liked, were ones who just hadn't been ground down yet. They were all people who had a very clear passion for their work and their studies and knew a lot about the things that they were talking about and had fun with it and were cool.

The things that BIS taught me were much more helpful than the things that any of the other schools really did, primarily in the fact that it taught me how to recognise the best ways for me to learn and how to implement that. I have ADHD and I get distracted very easily, so I find the best way for me to listen to lectures is have them on double speed while also doing a puzzle, because it keeps my brain occupied enough that I can process the information.

BIS really taught me how to recognize the best way I learn and the best way I write essays and everything, which is probably the most valuable skill, because a lot of state schools, you get taught essay structure and it sets up for lectures being a thing by having you sit in class for hours at a time in actual school, but that doesn't actually help people who don't learn well from that sort of thing. BIS definitely helped me the most with that. It set me up with the skills to recognise what I needed to do in order to make the most out of my tertiary experience.

[If every primary school was organised like BIS] I think it'd be really good. It's not necessarily just primary school though I do understand it. The education system needs to understand that standardised testing is ineffective. Specially standardised testing around stuff like creative writing and that's always been the most baffling thing around English classes throughout school, is the standardised creative fiction work. That's absolutely bizarre to be like, "No, you've done imagining wrong. You get an F." You can't hold everyone to the same standard, but it also needs to understand that kids are humans. They're not little drones who are going to sit still and do exactly what you want to, especially five- and six-year-olds. From that young age, those kids are going to be zoned out after about 30 seconds. You need to understand that kids are also humans and are going to process information differently. They're going to need different things. They're going to be at different levels.

If every school was more like BIS and recognised that fact, it would probably be a lot more effective in educating, because you would reach the kids better by understanding how to reach them better. That's probably what would be the most important difference, as well as probably improving the general mental state of students in terms of the happiness and willingness to attend school – if school was not something to be feared, something that was boring, something that was not helpful, something that was negative, if they make it into something that's more interesting and more tuned into them.

CHAPTER FIVE

Lifting the limits on growth

In chapter 3, we saw how support for consciousness development is built into the structure of most schools and is essentially invisible to those working there. We also saw how this support is limited to two stages – Rule Oriented and Conformist – effectively capping development at the Conformist stage, or at least discouraging or limiting development beyond it. However, in chapter 4 we saw how it is possible for young people to reach higher levels of consciousness development while still of school age – even reaching or exceeding the level generally thought achievable only in adulthood – and having a positive impact on the world around them.

In this chapter I want to show that these children are not isolated cases but rather represent the signs of a society-wide shift that will lift the capabilities and impact of young people and, therefore, over time, of society as a whole. I will demonstrate that it is possible to remove the limitations on growth and that young people are ready to transition to levels beyond Conformist.

Shifts in society

Today the adult population operates overwhelmingly in the middle tier of the STAGES model: that is, at Expert, Achiever, Pluralist and Strategist level. The Achiever level has the characteristics that are sought in effective managers and leaders in a modern society. However, as we will see, the developmental stage typically reached by adults has not been static; there is evidence to suggest that the level achieved by most adults has shifted over the past century.

Developmental psychologist Jane Loevinger considered the Conformist stage to be most common for adults in American society, based on her research in the 1970s, and thought that few passed beyond this stage before the age of twenty-five[16]. However, data collected from 1980 to 1995 by Susanne Cook-Greuter gives a different picture, with most adults then being at the Expert or higher levels.

The recently emerged 'Woke' culture which is causing such havoc in the Twittersphere[17] is based on the Pluralist level and possibly reflects that this level is emerging more broadly. Further evidence of this can be found in the growth of executives at the Pluralist level (at over ten per cent in each of the two decades to 2015), which puts about a third of executives at this level.[18] In recent years, Strategist has

---

16 Loevinger's definitions of developmental stages has been refined over time by Cook-Greuter and O'Fallon but as near as I can tell she was referring to the Conformist stage as currently understood. My own experience is that I transitioned to Expert at the age of about 26 and my father, who was headmaster of a secondary modern school in the UK, was likely at the Conformist stage his whole adult life.

17 'Woke' culture as displayed on Twitter and calls for 'de-platforming', etc. does not reflect the full richness and capability of this stage of development.

18 PricewaterhouseCoopers, *The hidden talent: Ten ways to identify and*

begun to emerge as the key level for senior leaders in various walks of life. Strategists can work *on* an organisation (with a fourth-person perspective) whilst Achievers work *in* an organisation (with a third-person perspective).

It seems remarkable that the most common developmental stage for adults has shifted by at least one level over twenty years; yet, I will argue that this reflects the trajectory that modern societies are following.

Are we getting smarter?

In the mid 1980s, James R Flynn examined the substantial gains in IQ test results throughout the industrialised world over time (later dubbed the "Flynn effect"). In his book *Are we getting smarter?*[19], he concludes that young people today are not more intelligent; just more "modern".

So, what is it that modernity brings? After much analysis, Flynn concluded that the ultimate cause of IQ gains was the Industrial Revolution. The intermediate causes are probably its social consequences, such as more formal schooling, more cognitively demanding jobs, cognitively challenging leisure, a higher ratio of adults to children and thus richer interaction between parent and child. More immediately, looking at the world through a scientific lens – understanding abstract classification

retain transformational leaders, PricewaterhouseCoopers, London, 2015. https://osca.co/publications/the-hidden-talent-ten-ways-to-identify-and-retain-transformational-leaders/.

19 JR Flynn, Are we getting smarter?: Rising IQ in the twenty-first century, Cambridge University Press, Cambridge, 2012.

and logical analysis – would allow more questions to be answered correctly (as compared with a utilitarian lens – where something is to be manipulated to advantage).

Flynn subsequently searched for earlier evidence that those taking tests in a pre-scientific age indeed saw the world in the way that he hypothesised. He found that the notable neuropsychologist Aleksandr Romanovich Luria had recorded interviews with isolated rural people in Central Asia during the 1930s who were still living in pre-scientific cognitive environments[20].

Here is an interview about using logic to analyse the hypothetical: camels and Germany.

> Q: There are no camels in Germany; the city of B is in Germany; are there camels there or not?

> A: I don't know, I have never seen German villages. If B is a large city, there should be camels there.

> Q: But what if there aren't any in all of Germany?

> A: If B is a village, there is probably no room for camels.

Today, we would say, "of course there would be no camels in this hypothetical German city". We are accustomed to using logic in such situations. The person whose life is grounded in concrete reality rather than in a world of symbols is baffled. Who has ever seen a city of any

---

20 AR Luria, *Cognitive development: Its cultural and social foundations*, Harvard University Press, Cambridge MA, 1976. https://www.hup.harvard.edu/catalog.php?isbn=9780674137325

size without camels? This is not due to limited experience but rather an inability to treat the problem as anything other than concrete.

Through the lens of a model such as STAGES we would position these rural peasants at the Rule Oriented level, a stage where we are unable to generalise (that is, abstract) an experience in one context to an experience in another, nor use abstract logic.

These Central Asian peasants from the 1930s may well have been the remnants of a much larger population with the same stage of development in the nineteenth century. Thus, it is possible that Rule Oriented was the common developmental stage reached by adults prior to World War One. This would match with education systems that used harsh discipline and rote learning for the bulk of the population.

We may conclude that in a period of not much more than a century, the modal or common stage of development among adults has moved from Rule Oriented to Conformist to Expert/Achiever and potentially to Pluralist today. I would argue, furthermore, that young people continue to develop at higher levels of consciousness earlier than previous generations.

Young people are ready to shift earlier

In contrast to those of a generation ago, young people today live in societies that provide vastly more stimuli than has previously been the case, with wide access to information – information technologies being a major contributor to this change. They are more exposed to conditions that spur the development of advanced skills than previous generations. This supports the case that young people are now ready to move into the middle tier whilst still at school.

Interestingly, two other indications that young people of today are shifting to higher levels of consciousness without appropriate support are the trends in mental health and academic output.

All transitions between stages have a period of being "down" – where what made sense previously no longer does, and what is emerging is not yet well enough formed to take its place. (It is for this reason that support is so important.)

It is worth noting that people have often been puzzled by the fact that students in grade six seem supremely confident and able but seem to lose all this when they move to grade seven. This is what we would expect to see in a transition – in this case from Rule Oriented to Conformist.

The transition from Conformist to Expert is the most difficult transition that most people will make in their lives as the three parameters all change at the same time: in moving to a new tier, the content of thought changes from being concrete to abstract (in the new level ideas, goals, subtle feelings are all accessible); there is a shift from the collective "fitting in" that defines the Conformist level to an emerging sense of an individual self, standing apart from the collective; and, the learning style is receptive, meaning that the person is "had" by the new thoughts and emerging self and cannot, as yet do a lot with them – they lack the ability to categorise or prioritise. This transition may take several years to complete.

If young people are indeed entering into the Conformist–Expert stage transition without the right support, then we would expect to see examples of depression over several years with a commensurate drop off in student learning and outcomes.

Although there has been no research that would identify stage transition as a cause, the following statistics indicate high rates of depression and anxiety in young people, especially as compared with earlier generations:

- The prevalence of major depressive disorder is higher in young people (12 to 17 years) than children (4 to 11 years), at five per cent compared to 1.1 per cent[21].

- In a 2015 report[22], almost one in five young people aged 11 to 17 years had high or very high levels of psychological distress in the previous 12 months; this figure rose to 36.2 per cent for females aged 16 to 17 years.

- Five times as many high school and college students are dealing with anxiety and other mental health issues as youth of the same age during the Great Depression era[23].

---

21 D Lawrence, S Johnson, J Hafekost, K Boterhoven De Haan, M Sawyer, J Ainley & SR Zubrick, *The Mental Health of Children and Adolescents. Report on the second Australian Child and Adolescent Survey of Mental Health and Wellbeing*, Department of Health, Canberra, 2015.

22 Commissioner for Children and Young People WA, *Our Children Can't Wait – Review of the implementation of recommendations of the 2011 Report of the Inquiry into the mental health and wellbeing of children and young people in WA*, Commissioner for Children and Young People Western Australia, Perth, 2015.

23 JM Twenge, B Gentile, CN DeWall, D Ma, K Lacefield & DR Schurtz, Birth cohort increases in psychopathology among young Americans, 1938–2007: A cross-temporal meta-analysis of the MMPI, Clinical Psychology

Similarly, PISA results[24] show a sustained decline in results for year nine students; again, what one would expect if the stage transition hypothesis holds true.

Supporting healthy development

Given schools' focus on concrete thought, which corresponds with the first tier of the STAGES model, the assumption implicit within the system is that young people are not ready to reach the second tier until after they finish school.

However, we now observe that young people are ready to shift stages earlier. Many primary-aged children are ready to move, for example, from Rule Oriented to Conformist before they transition to secondary school but, to quote Jen Haynes, Brisbane Independent School principal, "most schools will try and keep them at Rule Oriented because it's very convenient." Jen sees her students typically entering the Conformist stage at 10 or 11 years old. Perhaps even more important is that young people are ready to shift to Expert at fourteen, fifteen or sixteen years. Society needs them to make this shift, since twenty-first-century skills

Review, vol. 30, no. 2, 2010, pp. 145–54. doi: 10.1016/j.cpr.2009.10.005. Epub 2009 Nov 5.

24 The Programme for International Student Assessment (PISA) assesses year 9 students in Mathematics, Reading and Science in a way that assesses how well participating students can apply the knowledge they have in new ways. This is a good proxy for the skills required in the twenty-first century. Australia has seen declines in Mathematics, Reading and Science throughout the measurement period (2000–2018 for Reading; shorter periods for Mathematics and Science). See the following document for the full results: https://www.oecd.org/pisa/publications/PISA2018_CN_AUS.pdf

can only be acquired by people at the Expert level of development or above.

We have circumstantial evidence that the conditions needed for healthy development of senior school students have deteriorated and that lifting the limits on consciousness development – supporting transitions to Expert and even Achiever as young people show themselves to be ready – is a necessary part of providing the right conditions.

To support these transitions we also need to remove any delay in children moving from Rule Oriented to Conformist, if they are ready at 10 or 11 then helping them to make the transition at this age will allow more time to become robust at the Conformist stage and an easier transition to secondary school.

Assuming that Jen Haynes is correct – that children are ready to move into the Conformist level at age ten or 11 – this suggests that primary schools could organise themselves to have Rule Oriented environments (as now) to the age of ten, with the last two years providing a Conformist environment. This would make for a much smoother transition into secondary school and not hold back the emergence of the Expert level through stalling children's transition to the Conformist level. Brisbane Independent School provides transition classes (Egocentric to Rule Oriented and Rule Oriented to Conformist) which they find supports the transition more easily. Jen Haynes explains:

> When you're shifting from one stage to another, you will fall back swiftly into the earlier stage when you're stressed. So, when you pop an Egocentric early-Rule Oriented child into a solid Rule Oriented room where everyone is all about the rules and they're like little police.

If [the new student] falls apart and they start to have a tantrum or they start to demand their voice without any consideration of others, the collective will be very judgy.

Efforts such as social and emotional learning, curriculum with more abstract content and formative assessment are all supportive of children transitioning to higher stages earlier. The support for the consciousness shift is no longer coming from school structures but can come from the adults in the school: adults who can provide the right "holding on, letting go and remaining in place" behaviours described by Kegan. We know that around five per cent of teachers transcend structurally imposed limits on consciousness development, instead differentiating their response to students and providing support as transitions occur. These teachers – who we remember for our whole lives – show that this is possible; furthermore, that it is not disruptive but, rather, enhances the life of a school. In chapter 11 we will look at the implications of this in more detail.

In addition to supporting the growth in consciousness, it's important to support the growth of young people's innate drive for autonomy; as we will see in the next chapter, suppressing this has serious, negative long-term effects.

CHAPTER SIX

Counting the cost

"Ten years ago, we may not have envisioned that the number one issue facing our education sector would be the wellbeing of our young people and the adults who teach and lead schools."

Professor John Fischetti, University of Newcastle.

It's well established that schools support the development of competence; schools also satisfy our drive for meaning to some extent, by implicitly supporting consciousness development (even though, as we've seen, to prepare young people for heuristic work this must be more explicit and extend beyond the realm of concrete thought). However, schools have traditionally not supported young people to develop autonomy; instead, autonomy has been supressed by the use of controlled motivation (rewards and punishment) to control behaviour and, in particular, to induce people to engage in algorithmic work that does not require any autonomous decision making.

After World War Two, education was influenced by behavioural psychologist BF Skinner's theory of operant conditioning. Skinner believed that animals and humans learn behaviours through associating them with consequences. Behaviour could be shaped in three ways – through positive reinforcement (providing something good such as a prize or reward); negative reinforcement (removing or refraining from providing something unpleasant, such as humiliation); and through punishment (inflicting something unpleasant such as detention or physical pain).

In a world where algorithmic work is the norm, this approach is very efficient from a productivity point of view; and, although it limits the development of autonomy – and thus the growth of the individual – it allows economic activity to flourish, thus raising material living standards.

Yet, the use of controlled motivation comes at a cost. When we examine the longer-term consequences within a wider context, we find that using rewards and punishments to influence behaviour suppresses an individual's autonomy. This means that one of our innate needs is not being met. As we will see, this can detrimentally affect our engagement and motivation and, ultimately, prevent us from leading meaningful lives where we operate at our best.

Controlled motivation creates two mind states

Most of us recognise that we generally operate in one of two mind states: one in which we feel confident, collaborative and creative, and seek success – we are operating at our best. This state is often referred to as our "blue brain". In contrast, the "red brain" is a negative state:

our focus narrows, we become self-focused, defensive and tend to ruminate over past events. Rather than seeking success, we strive to avoid failure[25].

The red brain is essentially our childhood mind (where the lower brain is in control), which has persisted into adulthood. We no longer have access to the higher brain; we are very severely limited in our choices, in how we respond to the world and in our capacity to handle anything other than simple situations or tasks. We cannot operate at our best in this mind state; it is only in the blue brain that we can fully develop – and express – twenty-first-century skills.

So how does this relate to controlled motivation?

As children, our brains have not fully matured, which means that until around age 10, the more primitive parts of our brain are in control: we are impulsive, self-centred and can be overwhelmed by emotion. As our brain matures and our adult mind emerges, we start to leave the child mind behind: we develop self-awareness and the capacity for abstract thought and higher-order learning. We are no longer overwhelmed by emotions; we can make choices about how we respond to the world.

When, as children, we are rewarded or punished according to our behaviour, we construct a scaffolding around our childhood mind of "shoulds", "mustn'ts" and beliefs about ourselves that others have imposed. Rather than disappearing, the scaffolded child mind persists

---

25 My book *Red Brain Blue Brain* explains how the two-brain state has developed and is maintained, how it is no longer serving us, and what we can do to become our best – both as individuals and societies. J Corrigan, *Red Brain Blue Brain*, Sydney, 2019. See www.johngcorrigan.com/resources.

into adulthood (as the red brain) alongside the adult mind (the blue brain). When stressed or triggered we respond from these automated rules, experience the emotions associated with them and become self-focused. In this state our ability to learn is limited and our growth in consciousness is constrained.

To give an example, imagine a four-year-old (let's call her Jenny). At this age, Jenny's life is all about "me" and "mine": if she wants a toy, she grabs it and screams loudly if another child tries to take "her" toy. Jenny's mother tells her it is bad to behave like that and punishes her by taking away the toy. Gradually, Jenny makes meaning of these repeated experiences by accepting the belief that she is "bad" and that asserting yourself to get what you want is "bad behaviour". This belief has been imposed from the outside, or introjected, and is not the belief that Jenny would have developed herself.

When, years later, Jenny sees her own daughter behaving in the same way (which is quite normal at this stage of development), her red brain triggers and she responds with irritation, even anger, and repeats the process of introjection with her daughter. Jenny projects something she does not like in herself onto her own daughter's behaviour and the negative emotions that she had as a child now cause her irritable response. In addition, Jenny finds it hard to ask for what she wants in life; she can ask on behalf of others but finds it almost impossible to ask on her own account and, as a consequence she ends up doing what other people want. She was never allowed to properly develop her autonomy, the basis for adult assertiveness. In this case Jenny has introjected that it is "bad" to try and get what you want, and this limits her own life satisfaction as well as projecting this belief on to her own daughter, repeating the cycle.

Controlled motivation robs us of autonomy and thus contributes directly to the red brain persisting into adulthood. The problem with the red brain is that it severely limits our capacity to develop and express the behaviours that are needed for heuristic work, such as collaboration and creativity.

When we can choose how we spend our time and energy, our thoughts and actions come from within ourselves. We have fewer automated responses programmed into us by others, and we are increasingly able to ignore externally mediated responses such as advertising or narrative management of news broadcasts. With autonomy, we can be more creative – we can choose to think outside of societal norms; it enables us to think more flexibly – to be more open to new experiences and less judgemental. These capabilities are essential when it comes to addressing complex problems.

The long-term consequences of controlled motivation

The proportion of time we spend in each mind state, how readily our red brain can be triggered and how easily we can recover back into the blue brain, will all determine how we progress through life. We will seek success when our blue brain is dominant, and we will strive to avoid failure when our red brain is in control.

We can explore the implications of this by looking at how the consequences of controlled motivation play out in schools. Teachers, of course, were once students themselves, subject to controlled motivation in school. Examining how engaged and motivated teachers are, and the extent to which they seek success and avoid failure provides an indication of how controlled motivation affects adult behaviour more generally.

In 2017, researchers Rebecca Collie and Andrew Martin at the University of New South Wales investigated motivation among teachers, basing their study on the premise that protection and promotion of one's self-worth is the highest priority an individual can strive for that, in turn, drives two key motives: failure avoidance and success orientation[26]. These two motives align simply with the red brain and blue brain mind states which ideally suits our purpose.

The study surveyed 519 teachers across 18 Australian schools (including state and independent, primary, secondary and K–12) examining three factors that are considered adaptive and three considered maladaptive. Three wellbeing aspects were also measured: work enjoyment, buoyancy (the ability to navigate challenges and setbacks) and disengagement (a negative experience of well-being: the inclination to give up).

The adaptive factors – feeling of competency when teaching (self-efficacy), a desire to become more competent over time (mastery orientation towards teaching) and valuing teaching work – directly mirror the three innate drives for competence, autonomy and meaning.

The factors considered maladaptive were: anxiety, performance avoidance (the desire to avoid doing poorly or to disappoint others), and uncertain control, which relates to lack of clarity over one's role

---

26 RJ Collie & AJ Martin, 'Adaptive and maladaptive work-related motivation among teachers: A person-centred examination and links with well-being', Teaching and Teacher Education, vol. 64, May 2017, pp. 199–210. https://doi.org/10.1016/j.tate.2017.02.010

or about how to do something. Lack of clarity is a red brain trigger and an impediment to development.

Five distinct motivation profiles were created from the results: success approach (13%), success-seeking (27%), failure accepting (15%), failure-fearing (22%) and amotivated (22%)[27].

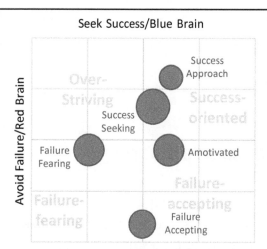

Seek Success/Blue Brain

The chart shows the relative positioning of the five identified motivational groups (circles sizes reflect percentages).

The positionings are indicative as they are derived from a simple average of the adaptive and maladaptive factors.

Note that the Over-striving quadrant is empty, which is not surprising, those with a high drive for success combined with a high avoidance of failure will often burn out early. It is possible that the unusual "Amotivated" group is the remains of those who started their careers as "Over-strivers".

Based on the quadripolar model of motivation developed in the early 1990s by Professor Martin Covington.

---

27 What groupings exist in practice will also be shaped by the environment in which people are doing their work and by the profiles of people who are attracted to, or recruited into, the teaching profession, as well as the attrition rate at various levels of experience (attrition rates are higher for less-experienced teachers than for more experienced teachers, for example).

Success approach (13%) – very capable and motivated teachers

These teachers have very high self-efficacy, value the work they do and have a strong orientation towards mastery. They are clear about their work and how to do it and have little anxiety or performance avoidance. They have high levels of enjoyment and easily bounce back from setbacks or challenges; they are highly engaged in their work. This group is operating largely in the blue brain and have their red brains well under control; they are correspondingly well adapted to and effective in their work.

Success approach

Angelica loves being a teacher; she feels she was born for it. After six years she has a comforting sense that she knows where her strengths lie as a developing professional and readily seeks out approaches and ideas from colleagues that extend her classroom practice. Angelica relishes the opportunity to get better and better, not for its own sake but because she gets great joy – and that is the word she uses – when she sees her students make great strides in their learning. The increasing amounts of research about how children learn, and the different approaches teachers use to get the best results, can at times be overwhelming and sometimes even contradictory, but she has learnt to make more astute judgements and not try to change too much in her teaching practice at once. Her anthem is that "it must work for the students" and her personal philosophy is that learning is about the long-term benefit. When a new approach meshes well with her students this fuels her desire for further experimentation and are a continual reminder of how much more she can do.

Success seeking (27%) – motivated teachers

Compared with the "success approach" teachers, this group has lower levels of self-efficacy; they value the work they do less and have lower levels of orientation towards mastery. They are less clear in what work they must do and how to do it and are less resistant to anxiety or performance avoidance. They have good levels of enjoyment but their ability to bounce back from setbacks or challenges is much less; however, they are engaged in their work. These teachers operate mainly in their blue brain but their red brain can be triggered by setbacks and uncertainties, leading to a drop in their capabilities.

It's likely that with empathic leadership and greater role clarity, this group would continue to develop over time to join the first group. However, without such leadership, this group may well continue as they are, well-meaning and competent, but not growing to their full potential.

Success seeking

Bianh had always wanted to be a teacher and is happy that he made it. The work is harder than he thought but he enjoys it and is determined to become a really competent teacher. At times he gets a bit anxious – especially with his year 8s – and, although he has planned out the lesson in advance, sometimes finds he has to limit what the students are doing so he can exercise control. Bianh feels very uncomfortable when there is too much energy in the room and worries that he is becoming a crowd manager rather than an inspiring teacher. Relaxing in a classroom with so many different things happening is a real challenge. Recently, though, he has started being coached and Sara, his coach, has really been helping in that regard, helping him to see the value in trying out new approaches by channelling his students' energy and helping him to feel calm which builds a relaxed atmosphere and greater commitment to do them. Sara is beginning to help Bianh see he is the conductor of the orchestra and that too much order is not helpful. Of course, feeling accountable for doing what he said he would do is another source of motivation. Last week he tried a new way of forming groups – he was so nervous – but it went really well. The coaching has been good as sometimes he can feel quite down if something doesn't go well; Sara helps him keep things in perspective reminding him he is not being judged and that teaching is very difficult – as is parenting – and, as such, is a real journey of growth.

These first two groups represent staff who operate largely in the blue brain; the first group, almost all the time, the second group having moments of red brain triggering where they will doubt their own abilities and consequently perform below their best. About two fifths of staff are modelling blue brain behaviours quite a lot of the time.

Failure accepting (15%) – little motivation to seek success but not too concerned about avoiding failure

Teachers in this group have very low estimations of their self-efficacy, do not value their work and have little if any orientation towards mastery. Yet they are not anxious nor performance avoiding, although they do suffer somewhat from a lack of clarity. The researchers call this group 'Failure Accepting', an apt title since this group recognises they have little motivation to seek success but are not too concerned about avoiding failure. Enjoyment levels in this group are the lowest in the survey and disengagement levels the highest. This group operates in the red brain – there is no passion or creativity and no confidence in their own abilities. Male teachers were more likely to be in this group than any other. It is likely that older members of this group have been using the same teaching methods for a long time with little incentive to change practices, even when they are not working well.

Failure Accepting

Edwin has been teaching for more than twenty-five years and has found the most recent changes really worrying. Edwin had developed a really good style of teaching where his friendly style allowed things to flow easily. As far as he was concerned he was always there for the hard workers, and got on well with the good kids, even if they were a bit slow – and of course the slower ones; well, what can anyone do about them? Edwin has become increasingly annoyed with this new philosophy that every student is capable of growth and members of the class should be actively learning – and can't quite grasp differentiation at all. He believes these new philosophies have a totally unrealistic view of human nature – not everyone can be good at these things. He knows he is nowhere near as good as some of the other teachers, or most of them if he is truly honest, not that he thinks about this very often, but how he teaches used to be the way everyone did. He rarely reflects on why things are as they are today and does not take kindly to anyone suggesting he could do things differently; he can be quite vocal in his opposition these last few years, especially, when some of 'these preposterous and quite unrealistic expectations' are raised in meetings. He has never entertained the thought that he might be fearful of trying something new, he just knows he is better off if things stay the same. His students know not to upset him, so his classes never get out of hand. He has the lowest results of anyone in his Learning Area – why do they keep changing the name: Department? Faculty? – 'it's all just change for change's sake!' he finds himself thinking about this a lot.

Failure fearing (22%)

Teachers in this group have high avoidance of failure: they are anxious, do not feel in control and have high performance avoidance. Self-efficacy is low as is valuing the work, yet they still want to get better over time. This group operates largely on the edge of the red brain: anxious, not clear what to do, avoiding difficult situations and people, avoiding taking risks such as changing current practice. They show little enjoyment or buoyancy – each failure hits hard – and are disengaged. It is tough being in this group and to move to the success seeking would require considerable coaching and support from colleagues and leaders. Again, this is a group operating in the red brain with periods of overwhelming negative emotion and self-talk, feelings of being the victim: the world is unfair, there is too much work, not enough time.

Failure Fearing

Danielle is fairly new to teaching and she feels anxious all the time, it was better when she still had a mentor in her first year. She would love to feel calmer and more in control, but she doesn't feel confident as a teacher and she is beginning to dislike the very thought of going into her next class. Teaching wasn't her first choice of career but still she would like to be able to do it well and her first year was OK. The trouble is often she is just not sure what to do and when something goes wrong, she just goes into a panic. She has become careful about doing anything new to the point of pretending she hadn't heard properly last week about the new strategy for providing class learning intentions, because she knew she wasn't going to do it. She really should share all these thoughts with someone, but she is really anxious about what they'll think about her.

Amotivated (22%) – just turn up and do the work

The fifth group, which represents more than a fifth of those surveyed is somewhat surprising: members of this group seem indifferent to seeking success, but they are not concerned about avoiding failure. They are not motivated by their work, which gives them no enjoyment. They are neither engaged nor disengaged; they just turn up. Interestingly, their strongest well-being measure is buoyancy: they can handle setbacks and challenges better than the success seeking group. It is possible that they seek success in other areas of their lives.

Amotivated

Carlos has been teaching for ten years and thinks that what he does is fine. He is a bit bored doing the same things every year but doesn't feel the need to change anything. He didn't realise there was going to be so much work in the job and knows what he needs to do and he does it, albeit without much enjoyment. When things change – a curriculum modification, for example

– it doesn't faze him, and he does what he is supposed to do. Occasionally, something goes wrong and, perversely, that gives him something to do that is out of the ordinary, so he doesn't mind too much, he bounces back. He feels no motivation to work voluntarily on his practice – "why would I?" – and aims to get out of school as soon as the final bell goes. He feels that he is giving a good day's work and sees no reason to do more.

Although this is not a demographically matched sample, the five profiles provide an approximate normal distribution and the characteristics of each group ring true to behaviours observable within the typical school. The two profiles that reflect healthy motivation (success approach and success seeking) account for about 40 per cent of all staff. Another 40 per cent have unhealthy motivation profiles, and the balance of about 20 per cent represents staff who seem to have little motivation: they will turn up to work with little investment in, nor concern about, success or failure.

Starting from a population conditioned to have two mind states (but in different proportions), we end up with a majority doing work with little engagement or enjoyment; this reflects that their innate needs for meaning, competence and autonomy are not being met. This is not the fault of the individuals concerned – they had no control over how they were being conditioned – but an inherent flaw in the system itself.

Sound familiar?

These findings are not unique to education (or to Australia[28]): research into engagement levels in the business sector shows a similar pattern. In 2018 Gallup reported that the percentage of "engaged" workers in the US – those involved in, enthusiastic about and committed to their work and workplace – was 34 per cent. The level of "actively disengaged" workers (those who have miserable work experiences) was 13 per cent. The remaining 53 per cent of workers were in the "not engaged" category: they may be generally satisfied but are not cognitively and emotionally connected to their work and workplace; they will usually show up to work and do the minimum required but will quickly leave their company for a slightly better offer. Furthermore, Gallup's regular meta-analyses[29] consistently show that employee engagement consistently affects an organisation's key performance outcomes regardless of industry or country.

In short, the more engaged employees are, the more successful their organisation and, we can infer, the more meaningful are the lives of those who are engaged.

The cost of conditioning our children to have two mind states has very

---

28 A 2015 Gallup Study in the US showed that 30 per cent of teachers were "actively engaged" in their jobs, 57 per cent said that they were "not engaged" at work, and an additional 13 per cent said that they were "actively disengaged" – that is, they "act out their unhappiness in ways that undermine what their co-workers accomplish". See https://news.gallup.com/poll/180455/lack-teacher-engagement-linked-million-missed-workdays.aspx

29 *Gallup 2016 Q^{12} Meta-Analysis: The relationship between engagement at work and organizational outcomes*, Ninth edition, Gallup, April 2016. https://news.gallup.com/reports/191489/q12-meta-analysis-report-2016.aspx

long-term detrimental effects throughout society – be it in schools or in businesses. It sets them up for a high likelihood of disengagement, limiting their prospects of success.

This is not what we want for our children, nor is it what serves us as a society. To get a different outcome we need to change the starting conditions: specifically, we must stop using controlled motivation – reward and punishment – which fosters the development of the red brain; instead, we must support the development of autonomy, thus fostering self-motivation. Ideally, this would start in the home but, if not, it really must start in school to repair any earlier damage and to prepare young people to operate as closely as possible to their best: in the blue brain all the time.

The conditioning of young minds through controlled motivation has long-term and pernicious effects. Its sell-by-date has well and truly expired.

CHAPTER SEVEN

Preparing young people for a future that's here

We now know that for young people to handle heuristic work, we need to shift from constraining young people's development to meet dated industrial needs and, instead, support full and healthy growth in all three innate drives.

Imagine doing carpentry using just a hammer. By adding a saw and a screwdriver you can handle a wider range of tasks, even the very big ones. Having more tools opens up the number of possibilities; it also opens our thinking: we can do more – and imagine doing more.

Heuristic work is intrinsically engaging as it makes demands on all three of our innate drives. However, it is not for the faint-hearted. We need to support students to be ready for heuristic work – to be capable of adaptive reasoning, critical thinking, creativity, problem solving, collaboration, open-mindedness, cultural competence, global awareness, ethics, digital literacy and more – the so-called twenty-first-century skills that they will need.

To do this sort of work, people need to be in the blue brain at the outset; moreover, they need to be able to continue in that state when things become non-linear and difficult. For young people to have this capability when they leave school, it's important that their red brain is not developed (or further developed) at school; rather, that school helps them to heal any existing damage.

Autonomy

We need to support the development of autonomy so that a child has some measure of control over how they spend their time and energy and is not fenced in by the "shoulds" and "mustn'ts" that conditioning through controlled motivation creates within them, and that become red brain triggers.

Rewards and punishments must be discarded as means for getting work done. In their place, work will get done by supporting the autonomy and self-motivation of students to engage willingly in their work because their work holds meaning for them. We will see in chapter 11 that teachers can provide such meaning for students so that they willingly do their best work, free of any rewards or punishments.

Autonomy is also the key factor that allows individuals to apply their unique strengths to whatever situation they are facing and so perform at their best. We learn and perform best where we can use our strengths[30]. At the brain level, we make more neural connections where

---

30 A 2015 study of 97 high performing teams, quoted in M Buckingham & A Goodall, 'Nine Lies about work', *Harvard Business Review Press*, Boston, 2019, found that the opportunity to use one's strengths at work daily was the factor with the strongest connection to overall engagement.

existing connections are most dense (which represents where we have developed the most – that is, our strengths).

Competence

Historically, schools have focused on building competence: initially, as we have seen, at relatively low levels for work that can now be done largely by machines; and, more recently, for more knowledge-intensive work. We saw in chapter 3 that the extent to which a person can become more competent is constrained by their capacity for more complex thought: for heuristic work, people must become capable of abstract thought and aware of subtle feelings (such as compassion, resentment or trust). This, as we saw, is only possible in the second tier of the STAGES model of development – that is, at the Expert level or higher.

In short, to develop the skills for heuristic work, young people need higher levels of consciousness than schools were designed to support, which then opens the possibilities to develop competence to still higher levels. Current developments in curriculum and pedagogy are already pushing in this direction; we now need to make support for consciousness development explicit in the interpersonal and cultural life of the school and develop adult capabilities to support students as they transition to higher stages.

Meaning

As we have seen, we can support meaning-making or consciousness development in two ways. The structural way is to have different adults support different levels of development either side of an engineered disequilibrating event such as a move from primary school to secondary school. Current primary school and secondary school teachers support Rule Oriented and Conformist levels, respectively. This has worked very well for a long time but is no longer adequate if children are ready to move to Conformist before they transition to secondary school and secondary school students are ready to transition to Expert or even Achiever levels before they leave school.

We can also support the evolution of meaning making by adults being aware of a child's need and supporting each of the three different phases. First, supporting a child where they are in their current stage of development (holding on, as Kegan described it). Second, noticing that the child is pushing their behaviour towards the next developmental stage and resisting the urge to hold them back (letting go). In the final step (remaining in place), welcoming the child back with behaviours that support the new level of development.

These are the steps we naturally do – however imperfectly – as parents of a young child making the transition from Impulsive to Egocentric. We let the child crawl, provided it is safe, and we go into raptures when they take their first steps. Because these are very concrete actions, they are easier to recognise and support than what may be happening to a child's behaviour as they shift from Rule Oriented to Conformist. Yet these are just differences of degree; it is a case of experience – learning the signs and characteristics of each stage and what support is needed – although it may not be so obvious as when a child is learning to walk.

Developing these capabilities, as we will see in chapter 11, is largely a case of paying attention to the child as a person in evolution rather than as a problem to be solved (the problem being how to tick off competencies within the required timeframe).

Remaking the system

We have seen that students live in a modern culture that stimulates – and requires – higher levels of consciousness, and that young people are ready to develop further and faster than schools were designed to support. Society needs this acceleration. What is missing are the changes in the schooling system to support accelerated growth in consciousness and competence and the healthy development of autonomy.

The key changes are in the personal and cultural life of a school; in particular, changing the relationship between teacher and student so that consciousness and autonomy are supported and space is created for higher levels of competence to be developed through a range of old and new means. For example, a "flipped classroom" allows the teacher to engage with students in class in ways that support their growth in consciousness and autonomy and a more sophisticated level of competence, whilst basic knowledge is acquired outside of class via online, audio-visual technologies. Opportunities for differentiated learning expand as student levels of autonomy and consciousness both increase.

For the students to grow faster and further, the child needs adults who can support their need for autonomy, their need for faster growth in consciousness and support their growth in competence beyond concrete objects of thought. As we will see in the next chapter, this adds up to a transformation in the role of teacher from, historically, "someone who teaches" to the much more valuable facilitator of growth, and role model for what it means to be a healthy human in the twenty-first century. Thus, adults must develop and grow to support their students: evolving their practice, evolving their behaviours to support autonomy and consciousness development, and becoming healthier and more capable in the process.

In such an environment we would expect to see children transitioning to higher levels of consciousness at earlier ages: moving to Conformist whilst still at primary school, making a simpler transition to secondary school, and moving into Expert within a few years of entering secondary school. We may also begin to see students transitioning into the Achiever stage (or higher) before they leave school. As we have seen in chapter 4, this is quite possible. Achievers are highly self-directed, which makes this the ideal stage of development to take on tertiary education in the twenty-first century.

Support for consciousness development would no longer be simply structural (and essentially invisible), but the outcome of meaningful relationships between adult and child, teacher and student. Creating an explicit requirement for teachers to build relationships with their students would put the current trend for doing so on a sound footing – clarifying the expected behaviours and dispelling any confusion about what is acceptable.

This is a differentiated model as children develop consciousness on no pre-ordained timetable and their strengths will be unique to each. Thus, secondary teachers would need to modify their behaviour according to what each student needs. They might have students at the Conformist,

Expert and even Achiever levels, with quite different abilities to build competence. Being quite a departure from the current system, such a change would happen gradually as teachers acquired new skills to grow into this new role. Chapters 8, 10 and 11 point to how this can take place.

Teachers, therefore, will also be learners, as they are now, and their learning will involve how best to support students to develop their consciousness and autonomy as well as how best to build competence. In turn, teachers will need support for their own development of consciousness and autonomy, as well as competence in their teaching. This support will come from school leaders who have gradually been developing their own abilities to act autonomously and their own levels of consciousness as a result of the pressures placed on schools by the changes in society[31].

---

31 I have consciously refrained from discussing the development of consciousness in adults working in schools as there have not yet been any large-scale studies to illuminate this landscape. However, I have some quantitative data that indicates that the consciousness of senior school leaders has evolved. The shift to a more strategic focus is an expression of this.

CHAPTER EIGHT

The value of teachers

In service industries the interaction between the provider and consumer is a significant part of the overall value to a consumer. Professions are good examples of this: it is well established that a doctor's bedside manner has a significant impact on the recovery rate of their patients, for instance.

The value gap in education

While working in the corporate sector some time ago, I developed a methodology to assess how much value employees create through their interaction with clients or customers. Nearly twenty years ago, I applied this methodology to measure the value that teachers provided to parents and students (and therefore indirectly to society).

The result was what I described as "indifference": that is, parents perceived the value as adequate but, clearly, teachers were not doing something that society could reasonably expect them to be doing. I describe this as a "value gap". Another way of looking at this is to say that teachers do well what they do, but are capable of providing something much more valuable. Teachers typically represent about 80 per cent of education's operating costs, so raising the value of this very considerable investment would have far reaching impact.

We all use services of many kinds – retail services, professional services (doctors, accountants, clerics, lawyers), and so on – and we judge each experience against others. For any specific service we make an (unconscious) judgement of its value compared to others; we determine a "felt value", which is what we respond to.

When our felt value is less than we would have expected, we experience a value gap. We don't know how to fix it because we only know what the service provider is *actually* doing, not what they *could* do. It is up to the service provider to understand the nature of the value gap and modify their service to provide something of higher value.

Let me be clear: the apparent value gap in education is not the fault of an individual teacher or school leader; indeed, as I suggested above, teachers do well what they do. The issue is with the system not delivering what it could be delivering.

Also, let me emphasise that this is not uncommon: many organisations deliver adequate (or less than adequate) value and only realise it when a competitor works out what customers really want and surges ahead by delivering this higher value.

Fixing the value gap – an example from another professional service sector

Before I became involved in the education sector, I managed a group of engineering firms. Consulting engineers had, on average, seen a halving of real fee income and salaries over the previous thirty years – somewhat like teachers, in fact. This was, in part, because of a gradual move towards a more efficient and cost-effective model of service provision.

The problem was that there had been a shift in client from the asset owner to the building contractor – the client's needs had therefore changed – but the firm was providing the service in the same way it had done in the past.

When the firm examined what their new clients' needs really were, they uncovered various reasons why their service did not suit these needs – which meant that the clients paid less for it. This problem was common across the sector.

The firm then changed internal work activities to deliver a service and process that worked better for their clients. After five years it had a return on sales greater than 25 per cent, more than three times higher than competitors. None of their competitors could understand why there was such a difference in profitability.

The lesson from this example is that, if there is a value gap, you need to find it and work out a way to create the higher value that key stakeholders reasonably expect to receive. Do this and you will thrive.

Teachers are key to providing greater value

The preamble to the AITSL *Australian Professional Standards for Teachers*[32] highlights the crucial role of the teacher, asserting that:

> "teacher quality is the single most important in school factor influencing student achievement. Effective teachers can be a source of inspiration and, equally importantly, provide a dependable and consistent influence on young people as they make choices about further education, work and life."

It also notes that teachers "account for the vast majority of expenditure in school education and have the greatest impact on student learning, far outweighing the impact of any other education program or policy."

These assertions are abundantly supported by evidence – and, for anyone in education, they are clearly apparent.

We know that the education sector could provide much greater value to students and parents. As we have seen, society needs students to develop higher levels of autonomy and consciousness while at school; yet the education system has largely ignored this need, providing little or no explicit support for the development of either.

The value gap in education could be resolved by teachers developing the capabilities to support autonomy and growth in consciousness.

---

32 Australian Institute for Teaching and School Leadership, *Australian professional standards for teaching*, Australian Institute for Teaching and School Leadership, 2011.

Teacher taxonomy

Supporting each of the innate drives requires different capabilities and behaviours. We can classify teacher performance on the basis of these capabilities and behaviours and use this classification as a basis from which to build teacher capabilities to close the value gap.

Competent teachers

Our current education system began with a focus on developing competence. Teaching was limited to concrete objects of thought and dominant learning strategies were memorisation and procedural repetition. Autonomy was not considered desirable and examples of it were curbed. Support for consciousness development was built into the system; teachers did not need to consciously engage with this aspect of development.

We can call the teachers in this environment "Competent teachers" in the dual sense that they focus primarily on supporting competence and that they tick the boxes for the system to meet its objectives.

After World War Two, the Competent teacher used controlled motivation to teach the curriculum efficiently and control their class. Punishment once represented a real physical threat; over time this softened to the point where controlled motivation was often not effective as a primary means of control, ushering in the need for relationships that engage and inspire. Yet those who remain as Competent teachers have not so far made this step.

The research discussed in chapter 6 indicates that Competent teachers currently represent perhaps 60 per cent of all teachers. The analysis in this study indicated that Competent teachers have little to no enjoyment of their work, and that their engagement ranges from indifference to deep disengagement; their feelings of competence and desire to improve are similarly low.

There is little chance that a Competent teacher will change their behaviour while student competence is the primary outcome of the system. This explains their resistance to any suggestion that teachers should change their behaviour, particularly since voluntarily changing their own behaviour would involve considerable personal effort. Yet, for their long-term health and wellbeing, they need work that is meaningful.

Motivated teachers

"Relationships, relationships, relationships!" is the rallying cry of teachers who recognise that students need more than competence alone and that some measure of control over their work is also necessary. These teachers recognise that autonomy improves engagement and encourages self-motivation (there is no need, then, for controlled motivation).

We might call these teachers highly competent teachers – or, in this taxonomy, "Motivated teachers". Students of Motivated teachers achieve better outcomes: they become more competent and are better able to direct their efforts to acquire yet greater competence and to apply their competence in ways that deliver greater performance.

Nevertheless, Motivated teachers still baulk at allowing students to step too far from the norm. Despite having good relationships with their students, they might for example, hold a ten-year-old back from transitioning to the Conformist level of development as the Conformist behaviours are too different and may even threaten the good order of the class.

The study outlined in chapter 6, suggests that about 35 per cent of teachers may fall into this category today. The analysis indicates that these teachers have good to high self-efficacy, value their work and are driven towards mastery. They are not much limited by lack of clarity, anxiety or performance avoidance.

Motivated teachers naturally modify their behaviour to better meet the visible needs of their students as they go about their professional work. Empowering students by supporting their autonomy seems obvious; gradual changes in their own behaviour come about as teachers see the response to their additional focus.

If the need to support meaning-making were visible it is likely that some Motivated teachers would also move in this direction as well. But it is not yet visible – other than to a small minority.

Enlightened teachers

About five per cent[33] of teachers have always had a lifelong impact on their students. Describing the components of the value gap gives a possible reason why: these teachers consistently respond with kindness and compassion to whatever their students say or do; students know that they will never be abandoned, so have the space and confidence to lean into a new stage of development. I call these teachers "Enlightened teachers".

Enlightened teachers support the development of autonomy, competence and consciousness. A relationship with a teacher of this sort is literally full of meaning for the students, who do not want to lose it or compromise it in any way: they will go out of their way not to disappoint or let down their teacher – leading to few, if any, discipline problems – and willingly do their best work.

Despite the memorable impact Enlightened teachers have on their students, they have been consistently few in number. This makes sense: there has been no requirement to support consciousness development in the current system and for a long-time autonomy was held in check. Teachers have developed in this way in spite of the system, not because of it[34].

---

33 This figure is estimated from surveys conducted on a demographically matched sample of 101 teachers in 2004, and a private conversation with John Hattie who proposed the same proportion based on ad hoc surveys of conference audiences. Data displayed most recently at https://www.linkedin.com/pulse/reflections-teacher-performance-john-corrigan

34 Interviews I have had with teachers confirm this; four common influences were: a particular family background, a teacher they wanted to emulate, a teacher they did NOT want to emulate or a mentor early in their career who pointed them in this direction.

Supports development of:	Competence	Autonomy	Consciousness
Competent teacher (~60%)	★		
Motivated teacher (~35%)	★	★	
Enlightened teacher (~5%)	★	★	★

A pathway to close the value gap

The level of consciousness development built into the school structure no longer matches students' needs. We have seen, though, that support for consciousness development can come from capable adults who are aware of children's developmental needs, alert to the signs of change, and skilled at facilitating transition from one stage to the next.

These are skills that can be developed. Enlightened teachers, though few in number, have always done this. There is no reason why other teachers could not learn to do it too – if support for consciousness development was explicitly accepted as part of their role. Compared with the structural support that currently exists, this would enable more flexible and differentiated support, which would increase the value of teachers to their students and, subsequently to society more broadly.

We now have a pathway for closing the value gap. By building teacher capabilities, all teachers could become Motivated teachers; with further development, Motivated teachers could become Enlightened teachers. Each of these steps would raise student learning and outcomes and increase the value of the teaching profession. Chapters 10 and 11 set out this pathway in more detail, exploring what it means to move from

Competent to Motivated (chapter 10) and then to move from Motivated to Enlightened (chapter 11).

There is no downside to having more Enlightened teachers in a school. On the contrary, there would be fewer discipline problems, fewer issues with parents, and far fewer problems that escalate beyond the level of the teacher. There would be higher levels of student self-motivation and better learning outcomes. Those students who are ready could move to higher stages of development, knowing that they are supported as they do so; this would reduce issues of student frustration and disengagement occasioned by delayed development. Higher levels of consciousness development would lead to greater competency in twenty-first-century skills.

Over the years I have often asked school principals: "What would your school be like if, rather than having five per cent of Enlightened teachers, you had 25 per cent?" The answer has always been the same: it would transform their school for the better.

CHAPTER NINE

A student's perspective: Case study 2

Alexander is a 17-year-old student in year 11. In this interview, he discusses some of his achievements and how he goes about reaching them, providing insights into the student–teacher relationship and how the emphasis on curriculum impacts on students.

At the beginning of year 10, I told myself that between the age of 15 to 20, I wanted to be in the running to get the Nobel Peace Prize award. The Nobel Peace Prize. And when I had built that goal into my head, I started to filter anything that would resist that goal, and I started to build onto everything else that would get me closer to that goal. So, when I had that big goal, I fantasised. I'm not afraid to fantasise, because I know my capabilities.

Most people think about short term goals and then long-term goals. I think about long-term goals, and then what short-term goals will perpetuate that long-term goal. I think about the big picture, and then what will perpetuate that big picture. So, at the beginning of year 10, I joined the student leadership group. I was a sports captain because

I'm an athletic guy (I do run for Australia) so, at that point, I was like, "Okay, this is the best way I can get into the leadership team." And because I'm not an academic person, I couldn't become a school leader yet, because I didn't have the credibility to be a school leader. Or, that's what I thought at that stage.

As a sports captain, I went beyond just creating sporting events and a school fitness club. I approached the premier, parliament, politicians who are making life decisions for us as kids. Because I felt like they needed to know, from a kid's point of view, of the challenges that we're facing, and how they can help.

At that stage, I told myself these people are always going to make decisions for us without asking us what should change. I was like, "No, no, no, no. I'm going to give you my point of view of what needs to change, and you're going to review that. I'm not going to review your survey; but you're going to review my survey."

I started off in March with a proposal for free public transport in Victoria for all students from prep to year 12. At first it was just something that I made in my room; it didn't really have the fundamentals of a masterpiece. I just emailed my principal, and I'm like, "Hi, I have this idea. This is how I think it's going to help the community; I really think that we need to make an impact in the community."

She's like, "I like your idea." But she told me to take a step back; I need to look at the long-term and short-term effects of the idea. I revised my idea, then went to my assistant principal, and showed him – it was now an action plan. He revised the action plan, and he's like, "Yeah. But you need your student leadership group." I'm like, of course, I'll be needing my student leadership group. I got a couple of students and, from there on, it was momentum carrying us. We all had this goal. We all saw the long-term effect; we all saw the impact we could leave on the community by just doing this in one year. By just prioritising this one thing, you can see the big effects, the big ripple effects, of this one thing.

We gave each other areas for study. I had the family-wise area: of how not paying your bus tickets can affect the family, and how it could really affect us when we grow up. Our goal was to get to school, but we got a fine getting into school. So, that was my area. And the other people took other sides: logistics and legislation. We all had our own bits and our own areas of study.

I didn't become the leader. This is where I became the servant leader; we all became servant leaders. I had the idea – everybody knew that it came from me – but even in the meetings with politicians, I didn't make it known that it was my idea. I made it known that we all had specific areas, we all contributed to this one idea. And that's how my leadership really kick-started. We kick-started in March with that proposal, and I was just doing more and more things on top of that proposal."

Alexander's background

Alexander attended a Catholic primary school, a 7–10 college and currently is in year 11 at a Catholic senior school (11–12). Here, Alexander describes his early years at school.

At primary school, I was different to who I am today. I was more aggressive. I was more arrogant. I experienced a lot of domestic violence in my household due to my father and him being so arrogant. Whatever he does, I do. It put this mindset into me that I couldn't trust anyone. I would have this arrogance that I couldn't trust my teachers, I couldn't trust my friends around me, and I couldn't trust the world. Because everyone had let me down.

At primary school I had teachers who supported me throughout that. I went to programs at Cassia, a program for kids who are a bit distressed at home, and who can't separate home life from school life. I learnt that I had to be open in myself. They told me that the best way to do it is to first assess yourself: ask questions like, how am I going? What am I good at? What is my biggest challenge? How do I overcome that challenge? How am I unique? And through those questions, I started to develop this mindset that I'm in control of how I feel, or the actions that I commit. I'm in control of the people around me.

From year three to year five, I started to transition into the person I am today, through the help of that Cassia program and the principal – she saw something great in me. One day I was in her office and she stands back and was like, "Do you want to become a philosopher?" I'm like, "What is a philosopher?" She said, "You like to think a lot. You like to think outside the box." And then, through her acknowledgement, I started to acknowledge myself. I was like, yeah, I do like to think outside the box. I am different to my peers. And that is okay. You're transitioning from this arrogant person to this person who likes to think outside the box, who likes to answer questions about life. Like, big questions: who am I? What is my purpose?

Alexander on his teachers

Primary school

The teachers in my primary school life just taught me for school things. They didn't prepare me for what I would face in the outer life, and when I grow up. They just taught me, "All right, it's the year school, you need to focus in school. You need to focus on this, you need to focus on that." And then, "Oh, here's the Cassia program. You should join this. That will help you with our time." That's how it was at school. I had the people who cared about me at home, and other people who just cared about my schoolwork. They would just make sure that I completed their goals. Every teacher had a goal for their students, and I completed the goal. I didn't really have a teacher who tried to break through to me, except the principal, who took time to sit me down and really see through me, through my arrogance and everything.

7 – 10 college

Look, I have to be honest. All the teachers from year seven to eight, they're really cracking down and trying to get students into the secondary mindset. They know that students are very restless so they would tell them all the rules, countless times. "These are the rules, these are the rules, and make sure you stick by these rules. You'll get through your secondary school properly."

From year seven to eight, I just had rules in my head, rules in my head, rules in my head. It was overwhelming for me because I couldn't really see myself in school. I was just seeing these rules, and I was obligated to meet these standards. If I didn't meet these standards, then I wasn't at the standard for life. From year seven to eight, I didn't really have a teacher who impacted me. That's why. From year nine onwards, I did. When I started to settle in, and I started to tell myself, well, I'm different to these kids. Yes rules, those keep me grounded, but I also follow the rules of life. Not just school.

It's a very multicultural school. We have a lot of Asians and Africans. I hung around a lot with the African group. They were really troublesome at school; they didn't really care about school, or about life, or their future. At that point, I was starting to understand myself more. And I cared about my future. I saw this quote that said, "You are who you hang around with." I was like, "If I continue being with these people, I will become like this." So I started moving towards the Asian and Caucasian groups. The Asian group were helping me with school assignments and my maths work and everything.

I started to accept everyone. And once I started to accept everyone, I grew. I wanted to know about people's stories and about people's lives so I interacted with people. I feed off other people's energy. I have a lot of energy and I have this charisma that attracts people. I would make them laugh. I would tell them my story. They'd tell me their stories. And we'd just have this interconnection where we both can just share our stories about our stages in life, and where we are, and the troubles that we're going through.

There were teachers that affected me in year nine. When they saw me interacting with other people and being different to the stereotype, those teachers were saying, "All right, this kid is different. He learns differently. He looks differently. He interacts with people differently."

And they started to ask me questions, like, "Who are you Alexander? What is your purpose in life?"

When they started asking me questions that I would've asked myself a couple of years ago, it really resonated with me. It made me feel like I was at home. And those teachers that made me realise that I was in the real world, not just the school world; they made me realise that the school world was just a little box in the real world. And I started having a better connection with the teachers who made me realise that life is bigger than just school. And their duty is to prepare me for life, not school. Because school is just something that prepares you for life.

Senior school (11 – 12)

I tell you what, secondary school is disgusting. It's all about VCAL (Victorian Certificate of Applied Learning) and VCE (Victorian Certificate of Education). VCE is the big bubble: we are all under VCE, and VCE is guiding all of us. "These are the guidelines, and this is what we're going to learn today. Here's the instruction. Get this done, or you'll be behind." That is it. "Get it done, or you'll be behind. You're not prepared for year 12. This is all preparation for year 12."

For someone who likes to care about other people and connect with other people, having that paper in front of me and having those guidelines, those restrictions interrupting you and I: it was affecting me. I saw a big decline in my effort for work. I'm six months into secondary school, and I already feel overwhelmed. I already feel like it should be over tomorrow.

So, I started observing how life at school works and how I could kick start my energy again – get that charisma back, and be a person of loving and care. I saw that what was lacking was a sense of community. Everyone knew who they were. Everyone had a purpose in life. Everyone said, "This is the university I'm going to." But no one was aware of the person to their left or right. I saw that. My teachers were aware of my work, but they weren't aware of me.

First what I did was observe, and I separated myself and said, "I'm not like them, and they are not like me. But I am no different to them, and they are no different to me. I'm a human being, they're a human being." So I made the first move with my teacher. Especially my religious society teacher. I remembered, at the start of orientation, she'd said that her father was ill and in hospital. So, last month I went up to ask how her father was doing. And she had this smile on her face. Like, "He is doing good Alexander. I'm taking him to the aged care next week." And I was like, "Good." And then we just had this connection. We started talking, and we started having this relationship that was beyond the school life, beyond the paperwork.

After I made the first move, she started to ask more about me and who I was and what I've done. And then when she asked that, I felt I was more open to work in the classroom. I was more open to show her my work. I was more open to work better, to impress her. Because now she knows me, now she knows who I am, and now she knows my life purpose. Wow. My teacher knows that. She knows how to help me. So, now I started to work harder for her, so that she knows that I'm really serious in this game. That it's not only that I want to go to the best university, but I want to achieve these things in life.

That's what I've done over the last two months. I think I've had a better, positive relationship with two of my teachers, because I've just opened up to them and they have, not opened up to me, but opened their arms to me. And yeah, so far, so good. But, it's hard. Some of them are grumpy every morning. They'll walk in with their suitcase, drop it down. "Have you checked out your notice yet? Have you checked out your things you're supposed to do?" And it's like, here we go again. One hour and 30 minutes of this again. So some of the time it's hard to go to my teachers and say, "Hey, how are you doing? How's life?" They look at me like I'm weird. Like I'm obscure. Why's he asking me how's life? "You haven't done your work yet."

I've tried to just smile more in my classes. When my teachers look around the class and speak to their students, I've been in the corner just smiling at them. And in a way, it has changed the atmosphere for them. When they know that one student is passionate about what they're saying, without them even thinking about it consciously, they will actually change their attitude. When they approach me, they will change their attitude just by me smiling. That's been working with my secondary teachers who're really confined to that VCE and, "This is what I need to teach you, and I'm the oldest here so I have the biggest experience, and this is it."

I'm a servant leader: I serve the people who serve me most. My teachers have served me so much. They give me so much knowledge. Without them, I wouldn't have half of the knowledge I know. So, I serve them, by just asking them, "How's your day? How's things happening?"

So, now the teachers are more aware of me. Without me even speaking, they're more aware of me, because I'm more smiley. So yeah, I'm planning to do this with all my teachers in a couple of months. So, when I go to year 12, I can say, "Yeah, we have a good relationship, don't we?"

I would say to any teacher, "Don't tell us the answer. I don't want the answer. Because I'm going to get it, put it into the exam and forget about it. But, if I know where to look, I can find that answer. I can also find another answer, and it's going to kick; it's going to have this domino effect. And my mind will be blown. You will not deprive us from the world, because my mind will be blown. I will see the world through my own eyes. Not through the teacher's eyes. Not doing what the teachers want me to see.

I want our next prime minister or next world leader to try to actually get the best out of every single person. As a leader, I feel like that's what I'm obligated to do. I'm not there to be authoritarian, I'm not there to be the head. I'm there to be the wind under your wings. But you have to do the flapping. That's who I am as a leader."

CHAPTER TEN

First, do no harm

"The true teacher defends his pupils against his own personal influence."

Amos Bronson Alcott

"The more certain kids are that someone's got their back, the more confident and autonomous they can be."

Melinda Wenner Moyer

What does it take to move beyond being a Competent teacher and take on the mantle of the Motivated teacher? Clearly, this about relationships. The teacher–student relationship gradually softens from being largely one-sided, in favour of the teacher, to one where the teacher no longer allows their internal impulses, moods or beliefs to dominate but, rather, keeps these out of the way. Thus, students can express themselves without fear of being humiliated, put down, ignored or made to be wrong. They have a safe space to formulate their own thoughts and try out the behaviours that follow. This is the space in which they can develop autonomy.

It is like the medieval practice of building a protective wall around a town that keeps out external dangers so that those inside can live freely and sleep soundly at night. It is the teacher's "shadows" that are the danger and only the teacher can build a protective wall to keep them away from the students in their care.

Within this protective wall students can try and fail without failure being condemned as a personal deficiency but as a normal part of the learning process. Students are free both to succeed and fail in their learning journey.

Ursula: A Competent teacher

Ursula is a maths teacher. She enjoyed number games as a child. One was a game she played with her father every Saturday as they caught the train. The train carriages had four-digit identifying numbers and they would try to make numbers starting at one from using all four digits and any mathematical operators such as adding, subtracting, multiplying, dividing, taking a square root, raising to a power or applying the factorial function (e.g. $4! = 4 \times 3 \times 2 \times 1 = 24$). She loved that game and could often work out a formula to get a specific number quicker than her Dad. She excelled at school, continuing to find maths fascinating and engaging and when choosing what to study at university, maths was her obvious choice.

She relished the harder maths in her university courses and could discuss the work with equally adept and knowledgeable fellow students, something that had been missing at school. In her final year, her tutor encouraged her to apply for a doctoral program, but she loved sharing her love for maths and thought that maybe she could teach it. She decided to do a DipEd (Graduate Diploma in Education).

Ursula has been teaching for five years now in a state secondary school with a solidly middle-class catchment. Her first year was a little rocky; not many children seemed to catch her spark but her passion for her subject earned her some respect and that helped her in developing an effective class management style. Not that she was naïve going in. She knew that many students found maths boring and difficult and she earnestly tried to make her lessons engaging.

Several students irritated her and her response, if they looked like they might play up, was to respond pre-emptively, raising her voice and singling them out. She did not notice other students sharing inquiring glances when she did this. In one of her year 8 classes there was a boy who really had an aptitude for maths, and almost the same level of love for the subject as she still had, and she really brightened up when he asked a question or handed in perfectly correct work.

Curriculum pressure meant that she had to move on to new topics before all her students had mastered the current topic.

She found that repetitive practice in solving problems enabled the weaker students to get reasonable test scores and justified this tactic by saying to herself that building this type of repetitive skill gave her students confidence, if not much grasp of what maths was about. It also reinforced a belief she had adopted from her year 10 maths teacher that some people just could not do maths.

Over time Ursula found herself focusing on the more capable students and managing those she believed "lacked commitment". "I'm here for anyone who wants to learn" she would often say to herself. What she didn't notice was how apparent it was that her attitude varied according to her perceptions about each young person. The students noticed that she was either warm or distant depending on "how conchie you were" and believed she only helped her favourites.

Ursula was satisfied that she had become a competent teacher; on her best days, a very competent teacher. Her classes were well-managed, and her exam results were, if not the best, still very respectable. She had the occasional complaint from parents that their son or daughter felt that Ursula did not like them but she strongly denied this; one complaint ended up being mediated by the principal and she was mortified by having to apologise to these parents when she believed she had not done anything wrong. She still felt resentful about that and had a twinge of feeling when she saw that particular student, but mainly she managed to ignore him.

Ursula thought that it was unfair teachers had to be responsible for students' commitment; "It's bad enough we have to teach some of them" she would often tell herself. "They want everything on a plate... When I was a kid I had to do everything by myself." The idea that she had to change her teaching practice to fix other peoples' problems seemed insulting to her: she had worked hard to keep everything moving along and felt it was unrealistic to keep the slow ones in cotton wool: "They had to face reality sometime".

She did not want to change anything much in case she lost control, the idea of which made her uneasy. When she was expected to try something new, she would go along but then not really do it, claiming that it had not worked that well for her. In truth, trying new things meant a reassessment of her educational philosophies and she intuited that this would challenge her own deeply held beliefs about the importance of taking responsibility, having personal standards and what makes a person a success.

By focusing on maths competency and avoiding opportunities to understand a more contemporary philosophy of education, Ursula has not focused sufficiently on developing her own teaching practice. Rather than seeing herself as "a mathematician who teaches", Ursula could grow to a new understanding of her profession as "educator".

Ursula has demonstrated she has many of the qualities needed to do this. As a young person she relentlessly pursued each maths problem, experiencing the unravelling of the solution "as a joy". To give her students the opportunity to develop the same autonomy she enjoyed, Ursula's commitment to being a dedicated educator needs to match her love for maths. Like anyone, she could have made this effort, but she has not done so: it probably never entered her mind to do so and there was no institutional encouragement to make this change – neither during her DipEd, nor at her current school.

The downside of a focus on curriculum

As a Competent teacher, the focus is on having a class that is well controlled and on delivering the curriculum as effectively as possible. Once an effective routine has been established, the focus is on maintaining this status quo. Internal impulses, current mood or beliefs influence the response to students (which seems natural, after all); yet it's common to restrain the same impulses in students and criticise some of their moods or beliefs as being unacceptable. When, for whatever reason, certain students (or certain behaviours) trigger a red-brain response, the focus is on avoiding the triggers rather than making the effort to remove them. This does not support the development of autonomy; rather, autonomy is suppressed.

To become a Motivated teacher, the key is to manage our own responses so that we are not triggered by what a student might say or do but we are able to respond always with equanimity. Is this easy? No. Is it necessary for our own long-term growth, health and productivity? Yes. Is it essential for supporting autonomy in students? Absolutely.

To continue the metaphor of the walled town, dangers are kept outside and inside the climate is one of equanimity, students who were previously favoured will still flourish and those who were previously ignored or undervalued can now also flourish.

A 1993 study[35] examined the effects of teacher behaviour on the behavioural and emotional engagement of children in grades 3 to 5 across a school year. They concluded that teacher involvement was central to children's experiences in the classroom, and that teacher support of autonomy and providing optimal structure predicted children's motivation across the school year. Researchers also found that students who showed higher initial engagement received subsequently more teacher support. They go on to say, "These findings suggest that students who are behaviourally disengaged receive teacher responses that should further undermine their motivation."

They provide two reasons for this last claim. First, that student passivity is aversive, which may make a teacher feel incompetent or disliked by the student; as a result they might like the student less and so spend less time with them. Second, passivity can be interpreted as a lack of internal motivation, which leads teachers to apply pressure to participate. They note that these responses to student passivity are seen across a variety of settings and roles and in that sense are dubbed as being "natural".

In short, a Competent teacher will tend to magnify initial engagement conditions; whereas a Motivated teacher – because of their internal work – is able to respond consistently and supportively to different levels of initial student engagement.

---

35 EA Skinner & MJ Belmont, 'Motivation in the classroom: Reciprocal effects of teacher behaviour and student engagement across the school year', *Journal of Educational Psychology*, vol. 85, no. 4, 1993, pp. 571–81.

Controlling the red brain is fundamental

We have all been brought up to have two mind states. The move from Competent to Motivated is about not allowing our red brain to be at all visible (or, worse, take over) when we engage with students. We model our blue brain, our best selves, keeping the red brain in check and out of the way. By this, we demonstrate that *we* can act autonomously: we choose our response – we do not respond impulsively or automatically. This is authentic adult behaviour: adults act with autonomy.

At the same time, by not responding defensively or aggressively or refusing to listen, we are not shutting down the student's own thoughts or actions. They can have thoughts or take actions that may be different from mine, and they can exercise them without being shut down or ridiculed. Other students observe this behaviour and see that it is possible to choose a response: there is no need to respond automatically or instinctively.

Ursula would ignore students she disliked (that is, students that triggered a negative emotion in her, which she interpreted as dislike). She paid less attention to them, therefore, providing less support. Students are astute enough to see what is happening and, rightly, interpret this lack of interest as a judgement on their worth. The student's self-worth drops, or they behave in ways to get attention – ways that are often disruptive.

In bringing the red brain under control we provide the space for students to expand their autonomous action. The teacher–student relationship becomes one in which the student is free to be themselves, not being forced or unduly influenced to conform or be something that they are not.

How to control the red brain

The first step to bringing the red brain under control is to recognise that we have one – and that it can be triggered by the presence or behaviour of our peers or our students (as well as by circumstances out of our control).

The second step is to recognise that this triggering is our problem, not a problem of the other person: if I am triggered, something in my past is driving the emotional cascade that is occurring – it is not someone (or something) else's fault.

If I withdraw in the presence of authority figures, my past experience is intruding to diminish my capability. If the way a student holds a pencil irritates me, I am reliving something in my past when I see this. Yes, people can be mean and unhelpful, but this may also be because they are affected by their past conditioning. Others may be triggered by my presence or actions, by someone else, or the environment in general.

A famous quote attributed to Plato (but probably coined in the 19th century by someone else) urges "Be kind, everyone you meet is fighting a hard battle" and is appropriate here. Through our conditioning, every one of us must struggle to present our better selves to the outside world. It is our better selves that is of most value to our students.

When the red brain takes control, we lose capability and perspective, and tend to become defensive in responding to others. In this state, our ability to support a child's autonomous development is much diminished.

To offer appropriate support to children, adults need to be able to maintain a blue brain state, regardless of what others say or do, and of what has happened before class.

The journey from Competent to Motivated is the journey of bringing the red brain under control and gradually extinguishing the triggers that cause it to take over. This will bring lasting benefits to the teacher's physical and mental health and allow them to provide greater value to their students.

The practices to control the red brain are well understood[36], but are not applied systematically in schools. Teachers (like all of us!) struggle to provide blue brain responses consistently, unless the management of their red brain is an integral part of their practice – which it is not, for many teachers.

What if supporting autonomy was a desired outcome?

Many adults, once they grasp the concept of having two mind states, recognise that they would feel and live better without any red brain triggering. However, most hesitate at putting in the effort required to achieve this.

In schools, around 40 per cent of teachers have – by whatever means – become capable of controlling their red brain and behave as Motivated or Enlightened teachers. But, because there is no requirement in our current schooling system to move beyond being a Competent teacher, there is little incentive for most to put in the time and effort to change their current practice.

---

36 My own recent book *Red Brain Blue Brain* lays out a series of strategies and practices to manage the red brain. See: http://www.johngcorrigan.com/resources

If supporting the development of autonomy was an explicitly desired outcome of the schooling system, structures could be created that encourage all teachers to move along this development path.

By learning to manage their red brain, teachers would have a greater level of personal control and would provide a higher level of value to their students. This will not happen through wishful thinking: to move a critical mass of teachers in this direction, an expectation that teachers support student autonomy must be built into the system itself.

The experience of those teachers who have brought their red brain under control – who already operate as Motivated or Enlightened teachers – can be used to help. Simply watching another teacher who has mastered this aspect of their practice can inspire confidence in the observer that they could do the same, as well as providing small vignettes of how to respond in a variety of classroom situations. This is even more effective when it is with students that the observing teacher has in some of their classes.

When autonomy is a desired outcome, a pathway to achieve this is for individual teachers to learn to manage their red brains.

Collective teacher efficacy – a key systemic change

With 40 per cent of teachers already operating as Motivated or Enlightened teachers, the environment is conducive to others coming to believing that the impact on student achievement would be significant if everyone in the school achieved this level of self-management.

This is collective teacher efficacy (CTE), which has one of the highest effect sizes in terms of its impact on student learning – and, in fact, the highest for any area that is under teacher control. John Hattie puts the effect size at d=1.57[37]. The most often used definition of CTE is "the perception of teachers in a school that the efforts of the faculty as a whole will have a positive effect on students"[38]. A study involving 47 urban schools demonstrated teachers' own sense of efficacy was higher in the schools that exhibited higher CTE[39]. Thus, CTE is a way to help individual teachers to improve their self-efficacy, in this case through improving their self-management to support student autonomy.

---

37 An effect size of d=0.2 may be judged to have a small effect, d=0.4 a medium effect and d=0.6 a large effect on outcomes. Hattie defines d=0.4 to be the hinge point, an effect size at which an initiative can be said to be having a "greater than average influence" on achievement. Effect size, d is calculated as d=(A-B)/STD where A = Pre-Test Score, B = Post-Test Score and STD = Standard Deviation of both samples. The effect size of 1.57 comes from a meta-analysis of 26 studies performed by Rachel Eells. RJ Eells, 'Meta-analysis of the relationship between collective teacher efficacy and student achievement', Dissertations, 133, *2011.* https://ecommons.luc.edu/luc_diss/133)

38 RD Goddard, WK Hoy & AW Hoy, 'Collective teacher efficacy: its meaning, measure, and impact on student achievement', *American Educational Research Journal*, vol. 37, no. 2, 2000, pp. 479–507.

39 RD Goddard & YL Goddard, 'A multilevel analysis of the relationship between teacher and collective efficacy in urban schools', *Teaching and Teacher Education*, vol. 17, 2001, pp. 807–18.

To help teachers adjust to a changing paradigm, CTE seems to be a key systemic change that can raise the efficacy of every teacher within a school. It is grounded in the same person-to-person relationship that children need from their teachers – relationships that are free of red-brain triggering. Developing these relationships amongst teachers is a key enabler for developing them reliably with every child.

Leaders clearly have a major role to play in modelling these new behaviours. They are more likely to do this when such behaviours are seen as an important and necessary part of teacher professional practice.

Opportunities for change

There are encouraging signs of change in this direction, although it is not explicit. A good example is the increasing use of (cognitive) coaching amongst adults in schools (where leaders hold themselves and their coachee in the blue brain while supporting them to exercise autonomy in developing their practice). Another is the widespread recognition that teacher practice is not static but in continual development, along with the increasing use of professional learning teams to stimulate development. A final example is the increasing use of student voice in general and, in particular, the use of student feedback to individual teachers to stimulate practice changes and move towards more mutual student–teacher relationships.

Pre-service teachers are ideally placed to build a practice habit of bringing their red brain under control. Not only will this improve their mental health and reduce anxiety; it is essential if we want to support student autonomy.

In a supportive environment with everyone around you striving to do the same, it is entirely feasible for new teachers to have achieved a great deal of control over their red brains after a two-year DipEd program – which would further increase as they are exposed to students and surrounded by teachers modelling what is achievable.

When the red brain is under control, a person spends more time operating in the blue brain, which makes them more valuable. Like any profession, the more valuable the work each professional does, the more valuable the profession and the narrower any perceived value gap becomes.

In summary

Teachers support the growth and development of autonomy in students by protecting them from the impulsive responses, bad moods and fixed beliefs that we have all grown up to hold. This is achieved by bringing our red brains under control and out of sight. About 40 per cent of teachers do this already and form a critical mass for developing a culture of collective teacher efficacy. If all teachers do this, the impact on student achievement will be substantial.

For this to be possible, student autonomy must be explicitly recognised as an outcome that our education systems are striving to deliver; furthermore, that bringing our red brains under control is a pathway to achieving it. When this is the case, it becomes possible to develop pre-service teachers to bring their red brains under control and present their better selves as a matter of course, and an additional impetus to systemic change.

This is the first change that raises the capabilities – and value – of the teaching profession. It puts teachers even more at the heart of an education system that supports and develops our children's three innate drives as they grow towards adulthood.

CHAPTER ELEVEN

Second, love is a better teacher

"Love is the only way to grasp another human being in the innermost core of his personality. No one can become fully aware of the very essence of another human being unless he loves him. By his love he is enabled to see the essential traits and features in the beloved person; and even more, he sees that which is potential in him, which is not yet actualized but yet ought to be actualized. Furthermore, by his love, the loving person enables the beloved person to actualize these potentialities. By making him aware of what he can be and of what he should become, he makes these potentialities come true."

Viktor E Frankl

The title of this chapter comes from an Einstein quote – "Love is a better teacher than duty" – and its essence is captured in the quote from Viktor Frankl. It is only through loving their students that teachers provide the ideal conditions for maximal healthy, meaningful growth to take place. Moving from being a Motivated teacher to become an Enlightened teacher is about building an affirming relationship with students which meets their need for being recognised, understood and accepted. In other words, it's about love.

To be clear, by love, I am referring to a *practice*; this is not to be confused with a set of feelings or emotions that we usually associate with the term. Love, in this sense, can be learnt by any adult and improved upon through ongoing practice. A necessary condition to learn this practice is that the red brain is under control so that, first, we are doing no harm to those around us, and we can operate most, if not all, of the time in the blue brain.

What does it mean to love another as a practice?

At its heart loving somebody is about how we pay attention. We have two modes of paying attention each of which has a different purpose and capability. *Focused attention* is about looking for what is already familiar; *sustained attention* is about being open to what is new or different.

Focused attention

In seeking the familiar, our brains compare what we are seeing (or hearing, touching, tasting or smelling) against prior memories to determine whether we have experienced it before. To do this our brains momentarily suppress sensory inputs so that our brain can compare and judge what we have just been sensing. Once we establish that something is familiar, we know what to do with it. Focused attention makes us very efficient at responding to things we have already experienced; it is what enables us to go into "flow" and solve problems or complete activities up to five times more efficiently than usual[40].

But, because the familiar causes momentary suppression of our senses, we can miss information that is new or unfamiliar – meaning that we ignore it. So, when we use focused attention, we may not notice something that is not within our scope of experience. This can play out in a classroom where a teacher may notice some students more than others because their behaviour is familiar and they can respond easily. A teacher may ignore an unexpected behaviour, signalling to the student that this behaviour is not recognised or deemed important enough to elicit a response.

Focused attention supports powerful learning when we work on a task at the limit of our skills and we drop into flow. The flow state makes us feel good about ourselves – it is meaningful – and, in it, we develop and refine both implicit learning and our capacity to generate insights.

An emphasis on rote learning, conscious memorisation and repetitive practice in post-war education systems encouraged children (and adults) to use focused attention as a matter of course, so it has become our default way of responding to events in a work or school environment. Television would elicit the same type of attention for those accustomed

---

40 S Cranston & S Keller, 'Increasing the "meaning quotient" of work', *The McKinsey Quarterly*, January 1, 2013. https://www.mckinsey.com/business-functions/organization/our-insights/increasing-the-meaning-quotient-of-work

to using focused attention at school, so its introduction in the 1950s further encouraged people to use focused attention during leisure time.

We have been so accustomed to this way of paying attention that it seems completely natural to respond to any event – circumstance or person – with focused attention. Essentially, we are treating events and people as tasks to be completed or problems to be solved based on what we have seen or experienced before.

Eckhart Tolle, in his 2003 book *Stillness speaks* says: "To reduce the aliveness of another human being to a concept is already a form of violence." When we use focused attention with people, we treat them as things, with no consideration for their unique perspectives and needs (which we may never have experienced).

What's more, they notice that we are not really listening to them (because, intermittently and momentarily, we are not) and they conclude that they are not being understood or valued; that they are being judged, even. This leads to a shallow relationship where the person feels no need to respond in any other way than in kind.

These were desired outcomes when our current education systems were set up. Simple algorithmic work does not need strong relationships: it needs people to focus and do as they are told, reinforced by rewards or punishments.

Using focused attention with students is not practising love.

Sustained attention

This second mode of paying attention seeks the new or different. It does so – necessarily – with a quiet mind: there is no comparison with prior memories and no judgements are made; there is no suppression of sensory input – we might miss something new if we momentarily shut down our senses. Because sustained attention is expecting the new or the different, we are not fazed by things we have not seen before; in fact, we notice them almost with a sense of wonder.

The difference between these two forms of paying attention is perhaps most clearly illustrated in the learning of a foreign language, which – to achieve fluency – relies on using sustained attention to expand the neural networks from which meaning emerges. When we listen to a native speaker using sustained attention, we pick up everything that they say, and new connections are made. When we use focused attention, we pick up on words we recognise and then miss what comes immediately after as our senses have been suppressed. We can get the gist of what is being said but we are not learning how to understand or speak with the level of nuance needed for fluency.

The well-worn observation that a four-year-old can learn a foreign language effortlessly and fluently yet very few eighteen-year-olds can do the same is an indication that our schooling systems gradually shift young people from using the two forms of attention in an appropriate balance to an over-reliance on focused attention. This imbalance is then continued in adult life unless an effort is made to bring sustained attention back into its proper place.

When we apply sustained attention to a work of art, a range of internal feelings and new thoughts can arise, which, in 1910, came to be called *empathy* in the English language. In the case of art, we recognise that we can be changed through its contemplation: a work of art communicates with us and that communication can change us.

This phenomenon is even more the case when we apply sustained attention to a person. Our mind is quiet, but occasional feelings and thoughts arise: we create new knowledge and insights when what we notice interacts with what we already know. We have the potential to be changed by engaging with another person in this way.

When we pay sustained attention to another person, that person feels really listened to and valued. More than this, they feel that they can trust the person listening; they begin to feel understood and that they can explore their thoughts and feelings in safety as this other person somehow "gets" them and their journey.

The response of those receiving this attention is threefold: their thinking expands, their feelings become more positive and they want to honour the other person by responding in a considered way. You may recognise that this describes someone moving into the blue brain.

A deep connection can ensue where both teacher and student are operating in the blue brain with empathic thoughts and feelings arising for both. Feelings and thoughts that arise represent new learnings or insights: for the student these may include the feeling of being understood, that they can trust this person; for the teacher, perhaps, the realisation that here is a new way in which a young person can be stuck.

Using focused attention, we reinforce what we already know; with sustained attention we awaken and build on existing knowledge to create new knowledge and capability.

Using sustained attention with students is beginning to practise love.

Use of sustained attention in schools

When a student consistently experiences sustained attention from a teacher, they so value the experience that they want it to continue and will go out of their way to try and maintain it – this includes trying not to disappoint or let down their teacher, and striving to do their best when they are given work to do.

Some years ago, I ran several focus groups with students and asked how they would respond to a teacher who paid them this type of attention. The students indicated that they would behave in the way I have just described. I then asked how they would respond to a teacher who had not habitually used sustained attention with students, but had begun to do so. The uniform response was that, once they knew that it was genuine, they would respond as to the teacher who has always behaved this way. Finally, I asked if any students in the school would not respond this way to at least one such teacher. After some consultation, the answer in each focus group was the same: every student would respond positively to the consistent use of sustained attention.

There are some indications that schools are beginning to recognise the value of sustained attention – at least implicitly. For example, it is the mechanism that underpins cognitive coaching, which is becoming more popular in schools. Sustained attention allows the coach to hold the coachee in the best frame of mind – the blue brain – so they can build energy and commitment towards improving their practice.

Sustained attention is also the form of attention that is used in the practice of mindfulness. With sustained attention we can become aware of feelings and sensations within our bodies. In comparison, focused attention cannot sense internal feelings and sensations (which is why we can ignore pangs of hunger when we are in flow). The increasing use of mindfulness in schools, for both teachers and students, is another encouraging sign that sustained attention is gradually being restored into the repertoire.

Becoming an Enlightened teacher

The shift from focused to sustained attention in responding to a student is the next step in becoming an Enlightened Teacher.

The first step, as described in chapter 10, is to bring the red brain under control so that internal impulses, moods or beliefs do not colour the response to students. Once this is achieved, responding to each student with sustained attention allows them to be lifted up into the blue brain; an empathic connection can be built and maintained, through which the teacher notices what is happening for the student in this moment, including what may be unique or new in them.

The third step is to respond consistently with kindness and compassion to whatever the student is saying or doing (or has just said or done). This means to respond always with a gentle voice and a desire to help the student find a way to move forward – or simply to acknowledge them: to let them know that they have genuinely been heard and understood, and that they are valued.

In responding with kindness and compassion, the intent is to increase the other's wellbeing or reduce their suffering. In practice, this often means to respond with a question – or a suggestion posed as a question – the sole intention of which is to help the student move themselves to a better place, a place where growth can occur. Because there is no other agenda, the student feels obliged to make an effort and respond by changing something – how they are thinking or feeling about their situation, or changing their behaviour in a way that will move them forward. The teacher's unconditional response is more demanding for the student, as it calls for the student to do their best; a conditional response encourages them just to do as they are told.

Using sustained attention and responding to students with kindness and compassion is practising love.

Gerald Bain-King

This interview, in which former principal of Christian Brothers College, St Kilda, Gerald Bain-King discusses the way he engages with students, illustrates the powerful positive impact of practising love as a teacher.

In many cases the reason a student would be meeting with me is because they have a concern or serious issue that needs to be addressed. Sadly, for students, this can be a challenging process. I remember, early in the role, having an experience that particularly helped me understand this point. It took place when I hosted some very high-profile old collegians in my office. And as we talked, I was surprised to hear their nervous confessions that they were a little uncomfortable because "they were in the Principal's Office". I quickly learnt that in a role such as this, you can naïvely confuse your self-perception of "me just doing my job" with what others may be thinking and feeling. This simple incident helped me keep in mind that, for most people, the Principal and his or her office can be a very intimidating space. And so, whether it be with parents, students or staff, I would always try to start most conversations as lightly and warmly as I could to create an atmosphere of positive regard and begin in the same tone to talk through the issue at hand, asking for their perspective – what/how things happened, how were they feeling? And still not shying away from other perspectives as we fleshed out the situation.

I regularly reminded my leaders to always talk to students with the kindest most interested voice because that's likely to elicit the most positive response and not a defence mechanism – as leaders you often forget what a powerful position you're in. In its own right, the conversation carries so much consequence, that you don't need to garnish it with a powerful or commanding voice as well.

With students, this process of friendliness and interested voice would usually generate trust and understanding. They would say, "So-and-so did so-and-so". And I'd say, "Well, do you normally do that with your teachers?" or "How does that make you feel?"

My goal was to make the conversation work in a way that would keep it open-ended and I was talking it through with them. As we had this exchange, they would quickly realise that I was actually interested in what they were saying, so they would usually talk with me – instead of having the attitude of "I'm giving him nothing!". I found that this way, when you demonstrate genuine interest and empathy, most young people are happy to take you into their confidence, because they want to be understood.

Because of this, I hardly ever had students just give me the "yes, no" routine. Most times, they would just talk to me and tell me exactly what it was like for them. Once I was able to do that, then I could ask them, "Well how's this happening? Why are you feeling so angry?" Or "Where are we going to go from here?" – whatever it may be. The subtext was always "I'm concerned for you – and the whole situation". They would know that I was concerned – and I was concerned. My own teen years were quite difficult, so I know how it feels for life to be not unfolding in the right way.

So you don't judge – that's the critical thing: being interested and concerned is the key. Once they sense this through your body language, your tone of voice, the questions you ask, they know it's not a put-on, with just more words, or you're not doing a number on them, or whatever. When it's not like that, then they won't buy in. You have to be genuinely interested and concerned about them and then they'll tell you just about everything. Because, more than anything they want care and understanding

– and the precious hope that there may be a way through it all. Of course, nothing is completely straightforward, but I found most young people always left a trail for me to follow. For young people, sometimes they don't want to tell you certain things, but they can't help telling you because they need to. Terrible things can happen in some people's young lives and this can cause embarrassment, guilt and shame; especially in circumstances where young people are being abused or badly neglected at home and they desperately need to have somebody know that this is happening. But it's so hard trusting and talking.

Having had the advantage of my own troubled times meant that I didn't judge them. As part of this, I knew that sometimes a particular question would talk to their situation and build trust, because they knew I understood – and they could feel safe with me because I appreciated their circumstances. It's a case of them coming to an understanding that "I can trust this person – they understand".

This understanding is not being permissive but having the knowledge that there's more to them than "the problem". And it's not that "he knows..." because I don't fully know what's happening to them, but they know I know enough to be able to listen and reach out; and that I am prepared to draw on my experiences to understand – that, one way or another, "something like this might have happened to him as well". Then they don't feel so alone and wretched. And this happens without me needing to share anything about myself. The questions tell them "he knows and understands".

It is like you're just trying to be with them and hoping to – when I say "guide them", I don't mean you don't have an outcome in mind, but you have the bushcraft to help them forge a path through. And of course, you both know there are responsibilities; in these conversations you don't stop being the Principal. So, should I discover that the person has been abused, at some point in the conversation you're going to have to talk about that – there are obligations you must fulfill – but it's the open-ended nature of the conversation and that you are comfortable working your way through this terrain with them, that makes it possible.

I remember it was similar when I was an art teacher because, before teaching, I had been a practitioner – an artist. Therefore, when I spoke to the students about their creative process, again, it was not a case of imposing a practice upon them, but just mulling it over and talking and exploring with them. They learnt I had been in this fix too or had had a breakthrough like this too. They knew they were on a journey with somebody who had been on their own journey, and that I cared, and that creates trust.

I have seen many art teachers basically have every person in their classes produce virtually the same style of art, with the only differentiation coming from the varying degrees of student competency. It was like Wedgwood China - a house brand that they all did in that class; consequently, they would often get great marks at VCE [Victorian Certificate of Education] because it was well honed and proficient. Whereas for me, a style of art is particular to each student and, as such, each is on their own particular journey of discovery with their own voice, and things to say.

I had similar experiences as a Religion teacher, in as much that, as an adult, I was on my own faith journey – and that's a complex business. I often thought, how hard would it be to be a Religion teacher and not be on that journey yourself? Because, in the end, your role is to not be giving the kids a formula. A faith is not a set of rigid propositions. Making sense of having a faith as best you can is complex and diverse – even contradictory. Students need you to open up questions and present faith as that journey of discovery: about what life is about (or isn't) and where there is sacredness, and how this one particular story and tradition can open up a particular understanding of what it is to be human. That's a glorious and wonderful thing. A teacher who understands the process of learning because they're doing that learning too can go on that journey with the students. And part of a teacher's learning is learning how to lead and develop young people through this exploration. When they sense that and can see you're not telling them what to think and what to believe, (because you wouldn't accept that for yourself); that you're here to help them explore these things together, then they go with you. I think it's the same teaching any area. You're their guide on this journey – their journey, not yours.

In summary

The main change in the journey from Motivated to Enlightened teacher is the shift from responding to people with focused attention to responding with sustained attention. Rather than approaching a student or colleague as a familiar problem to be solved or task to be completed, an Enlightened teacher treats them as people, to whom they are in service – thus, the teacher is open to the new or unfamiliar. In this capacity, they respond with kindness and compassion, whatever the other says or does.

The effect is that students go out of their way not to disappoint or let down the teacher and willingly do their best; there are no discipline issues, above average outcomes, self-motivated students and the complete absence of controlled motivation.

A pre-condition is that the teacher has already brought their red brain largely under control and extinguished most or all the triggers that they come across in their professional life, which means that they can look at, and work with, any student or colleague with equanimity.

The practices for moving from focused to sustained attention are well known – mindfulness and cognitive coaching, are examples – and already used in some schools. But there is potential for far more value to be gained. Widespread use of sustained attention would create the ideal conditions for students to continue their search for meaning and lean into their next stage of development with the confidence that their teachers are supporting them.

CHAPTER TWELVE

No downsides to being Enlightened

At the beginning of this book, I presented two questions that had hung in the air for almost 20 years: why don't all teachers behave like Enlightened teachers; and why do these behaviours matter to students (and, indeed, other adults)?

Why don't all teachers behave like Enlightened teachers?

In answering the first question, I have shown that the education systems that have been in place since World War Two did not require these behaviours of teachers. It takes effort to acquire and practice these behaviours and, with no requirement to do so, few have. Indeed, Enlightened teachers have developed *despite* the system, not because of it. Nevertheless, such teachers have an impact well beyond their modest numbers (maybe five per cent of all teachers). There are no downsides to having more of them.

Why do these behaviours matter?

The answer to the second question has been the major thread running through this book. These behaviours matter because they provide what a young person needs. In attending to each of our three innate needs, an Enlightened teacher facilitates healthy growth, development and learning suited to a twenty-first-century society.

The twentieth-century education model has served the needs of society very well for 70 years, preparing young people to perform the predominantly algorithmic work that has generated a good standard of living in modern societies.

In the twenty-first century, however, the nature of work is increasingly shifting from algorithmic to heuristic: technological advances mean that the work that schools traditionally prepared people to do is now increasingly being done by offshore workers and, more particularly, artificial intelligence.

Perhaps more importantly, in the twenty-first century, humanity faces existential threats – largely as a consequence of modern societies having learnt so successfully to exploit resources to increase living standards. Resolving these complex existential problems – even partially – will require us to work heuristically, and to employ twenty-first-century skills including creativity, collaboration and others listed in the table in chapter 1.

The twentieth-century education model no longer serves twenty-first-century needs. We have seen that the use of controlled motivation suppresses autonomy and causes the child mind (red brain) to persist into adulthood, and that this compromises our ability to develop and use twenty-first-century skills.

We now need an education model characterised by a teacher–student relationship that supports the development of all three innate drives so that young people emerge into adulthood with a full range of human capabilities.

The power of meaningful relationships

To be healthy, functioning people, we need to feel good about ourselves; we need to feel that our time and energy is spent in meaningful ways. To achieve that as we are growing and finding our way, we need a meaningful relationship with at least one adult (more, ideally) that is consistent and extends over a period of time.

In a meaningful relationship, we feel listened to, valued, understood. We know that whatever we say or do, we will not be ignored or rejected; we will always be treated with kindness and compassion. Because we want such relationships to continue, we respond with consideration – no messing about or being disruptive – and willingly do our best work; we do not need any reward or threat of punishment. Behaving in this way is highly meaningful to us. We feel good about ourselves.

Teachers are perfectly positioned to offer such relationships to young people; doing so adds value to a teacher's customary role of supporting students to acquire knowledge and skills. To add this valuable service, a teacher needs to have developed their own self-management to a high degree and shifted how they engage with students from a problem focus to a person focus by changing how they pay attention. When done successfully, teachers reach the level of Enlightened teacher.

Enlightened teachers are transformative

Enlightened teachers help students get into flow and to spend a longer time in that state, increasing their learning. When students feel valued and understood they can move into the mind state where they can focus on the work in hand without being interrupted by anxieties or worries. In the flow state we can be up to five times more productive than otherwise.

An Enlightened teacher can engage freely and openly with students and colleagues. Moods and belief systems are kept in the background and red brain triggers have been successfully extinguished. They pay attention to those around them as people to be respected and honoured, and they are eager to participate in the experiences, feelings and thoughts that students and colleagues bring to the interaction when they are fully listened to.

They have a high level of confidence in their own competence with a strong drive towards mastery, which is what has allowed them to achieve such high levels of self-management. Once they pay full attention to students as people, the true magic occurs: discipline issues fall away, self-motivation rises and being surrounded by young people is the absolutely best place to be.

Every one of us is imperfect. It is through engaging with others freely, openly and warmly that we become smarter, healthier and that bit closer to our best selves[41]. Not only is the environment that Enlightened teachers create great for their students; it is also ideal for the teacher's own continued growth.

Their positive impact on others gives Enlightened teachers incentive and freedom to continue improving their professional capacity; we have more time and energy when we are less anxious, less self-critical, less self-focused and ruminate less. Put another way, we are more energetic and forward looking in the blue brain than in the red brain. Such teachers have few discipline problems and few issues with parents; rather, parents are inspired. This, too, means time can be spent productively, rather than restoring failings or misunderstandings.

When large numbers of young people are guided by Enlightened teachers as they develop, we as a society, could expect to see improvements in mental health and self-esteem, as well as improved competence, confidence and engagement. We could therefore expect to see costs to society (associated with mental health issues and crime, for example) reduced as a result of the increasing value that teachers provide. This, in turn, would encourage further investment in this direction, leading to rising salaries, and increasing status of teachers.

Having more Enlightened teachers would not only reduce the costs to society: it would create greater value. By learning to operate in the blue

---

41 In his recent book *Humankind* (Bloomsbury Publishing, 2020), Rutger Bregman makes the case that *Homo sapiens* became smarter than other human species because its members were friendlier to each other, leading to larger brains and a greater capacity to share ideas and innovations. He also makes the case that humans still prefer being friendly and collaborative and that it is current and former institutional arrangements that have made us believe otherwise.

brain and developing higher levels of consciousness and autonomy, young people are more likely to work creatively, take responsibility for their work (thus, require less "management"), and are less likely to be swayed by external influences (such as peer pressure and advertising, for example). They're more likely to be collaborative and develop meaningful and productive relationships with family, friends and colleagues, which would promote effective teamwork and greater lifelong learning.

Being free to develop in consciousness means that young people would increase their capacity to handle the world's complexity; thus, we're likely to see the trend in human consciousness continue to rise to levels that enable us to face complex and existential threats such as climate change and resource depletion. In short, developing more Enlightened teachers would increase society's resilience and strengthen our ability to shape society to live successfully within our planet's physical constraints.

No downsides

More Enlightened teachers is a winning situation from anybody's point of view.

For the Enlightened teacher

There is no downside for a teacher to being healthier and more capable of creating the conditions for balanced growth and self-motivation in students. An Enlightened teacher's time and energy is used in meaningful ways, which makes them healthier and more valuable to their students. The more meaning in our lives, the happier we become. We could say that such teachers are providing great value for their students, their colleagues, society as a whole and for themselves.

Effort is required to get to this level of capability, however – as it is to develop other capabilities required to teach. Every profession has a body of knowledge and a repertoire of skills and behaviours that must be mastered. The teaching profession of the twenty-first century (versus that of the twentieth), will require additional knowledge, skills and behaviours to be mastered because the world is changing – and how we educate children must change too. The payoff will be a more valuable profession and more capable teachers.

For schools

From a school's perspective, there is no downside to employing more Enlightened teachers. The school would have fewer issues with students and parents and less internal conflict between members of staff. Leaders would have to intervene in fewer issues and so could focus on higher value work. Enlightened teachers have little, if any, performance avoidance and will buy into and implement practice improvements that will benefit students. Enlightened teachers are also self-managing; they require much less supervision than a typical Competent teacher, which frees leaders to focus on forward-looking issues rather than on day-to-day management.

Schools would come to embody students working hard on their learning, and teachers working hard on *their* learning. They would become true learning environments, the synergy created by the student–teacher relationship powering a level of learning for both that exceeds what either could do on their own.

For parents

From a parent's viewpoint, you can never have enough Enlightened teachers. These teachers inspire their children to become better versions of themselves across the whole range of human behaviour, making the parents' lives easier and their children's journey to adulthood that bit less difficult. More Enlightened teachers may begin to affect parents' own behaviours, as they become role models for how best to shepherd a young person through to adulthood.

Build Enlightened teachers into the system

There is no downside to having more Enlightened teachers – but, to have them we need to encourage the behavioural changes that they embody. This requires a system change. It is hard to do the work to become an Enlightened teacher on your own. Yet a small minority of people have always done it (despite the system). Now is the time for the system to recognise that the knowledge, skills and behaviours of Enlightened teachers are critical, and that we need to support all teachers to develop these capabilities.

Society needs young people to thrive and contribute effectively in the modern world. Fostering students' healthy growth and development of twenty first-century skills must therefore be a key goal of our education systems. We have seen how this goal can be achieved through the skill and approach of Enlightened teachers.

When the education system recognises that Enlightened teachers are the way to achieve this goal, an expectation can emerge within the profession that the Enlightened teacher is the norm. This book has outlined a two-step pathway that could be built into the system so that all teachers are explicitly expected – and supported – to develop the capabilities of Enlightened teachers. Collective teacher efficacy would reinforce this culture, so that teachers would develop their skills because of the system rather than despite it.

In the system change I have described, we would not, initially, see many visible changes in how schools are organised; nor much modification in the structure of the school day. These changes would occur later when there is a critical mass of Enlightened teachers who, collectively, begin to bring organisation and structure more in line with their new culture.

Enlightened teachers will become the professionals who shape education to meet student and societal needs. The priority will be behaviours that fully support healthy student growth, ahead of structure and organisation. Form follows function[42]: if we are clear about the function that is education in our modern age, then its form will follow.

Seventy years ago, teachers were employees of an education system

---

42 This philosophy, originally applied to architecture (the phrase was coined by the architect Louis Sullivan in 1896), is now used widely in other areas including modern organisational design.

over which they had little control, but which matched, more or less, what society needed. Now society needs something quite different and, to provide this different outcome, teachers themselves are in control. It is only they who can change their own behaviours and deliver the considerable extra value that society is looking for, which students need, and which will also enrich their own lives.

At long last, the teaching profession – in trusted relationships with students – will take the lead in forming, re-forming and transforming our education systems (and, indeed, our society) for the better.

Not a moment too soon.

APPENDIX:

Descriptions of developmental levels in the STAGES model

The STAGES model of development[43] developed by Terri O'Fallon maps the development of consciousness through childhood and beyond, describing how people think, feel and behave at different stages of development. The following descriptions, based on the STAGES model, outline the developmental levels in the first two tiers of the model.

The three descriptors in the heading of each stage refer to the object of thought (concrete or subtle), the level of social consciousness (individual or collective), and learning style (receptive, active, reciprocal or interpenetrative).

---

43 https://www.stagesinternational.com

Impulsive (1.0) – Early first-person perspective – Concrete | Individual | Receptive

Babies are born helpless. Healthy attachment to their parent(s) is a primary task for the Impulsive stage so that core needs are met. The crucial parental task is to provide a safe, loving and engaged environment for the child: lots of eye contact, touches, hugging, baby talk, sounds of reassurance and responsiveness.

Information comes in through the senses – sight, hearing, touch, taste, smell and movement – and, with vast amounts of trial and error, infants begin to discover their concrete individual self: where "I" stops and "not-I" begins. The taste buds are the primary sensory input for the first months of life, sensing new tastes, textures and smells. Interaction with food becomes a powerful part of self forming. In time, the senses mature enough to work together, and the baby discovers its own hand. In parallel, the proprioceptive network and interoceptive networks continue to feed immense amounts of information and responses so limbs, organs and systems learn to function independently.

The reflexive responses of attraction or repulsion are raw and unhindered by social niceties. The first exploration into moral development is drawn from a cause-and-effect reaction. Those around them give them language and reactions to these experiences that formulate their first labelling of their world.

Gradually, a baby awakens to their interior emotions: sad, glad, mad, surprise, and startle. By the time the baby understands what is its own body and that it can control when and how it moves, it is moving to the next developmental level. This occurs at about 18 months old.

Egocentric (1.5) – Late first-person perspective – Concrete | Individual | Active

Egocentrics are emerging from an environment where the world met their every need, and they continue to believe that the world wants them to have what they want. They do not understand that others see differently than they do, so at times it appears that they "lie", but do not yet know what "lying" is. When they take something away from someone, they have no remorse because they cannot experience what the other person might be feeling.

Interior senses are still quite immature, so it is hard for them to predict – to visualise – consequences for their behaviour, or remember and learn from their past. Yet they can visualise, talk to themselves and have their own feelings and wants. They may appear dominating or coercive; they get what they want and take what is already "theirs". They engage in parallel play with others, they prefer the toy to the friend and talk "at" not "with" other people. Event pairing also occurs, supporting often delightful magical thinking e.g. a lucky charm.

They are totally entranced by how amazing they are and what they can do. They believe they know why things work the way they do, having concocted a vast array of reasonings around this to fit. They are learning how to harness the amazing self to create and communicate. Often children at this stage will use a grammar that has developed logically from the grammar being used around them, for example, "sayed" and "thinked". Invented spelling also occurs and if you cannot read their spelling then there is something wrong with you!

They are listening and watching all the time and will role-play what the adult world is doing. The word "why" is the ever-present magic phrase of the Egocentric stage, eliciting focus and response from most adults and providing words to explain the world around them. A healthy Egocentric child will be building their world model on top of what an adult has given them, fleshing out the "truth" as they see fit, whether or not it actually relates to what they have been told.

Reliance on external senses still predominates and hyper-vigilance allows for intuitive manipulation, through various categories – physical (grabbing what they want), intellectual (being tricky), emotional (tantrums) and social (calling on others to intervene). An increasing ability to act in the world follows the stages of empowerment: the recognition that they have choice (autonomy), the capacity to take the first step to act on that choice (initiative), the capacity to sustain effort to make it through whatever gets in the way (follow-through), the ability to actually complete the project to finish and say "this is done" (completion) and, the ability to rejoice in the completion of the task (celebration). Think a toddler pushing a chair to climb up on to a benchtop to grab a cookie.

Exploring the world builds gross motor skills, a fundamental precursor to fine motor control, allowing them to discover what their body can do and how to control and hone it. They are incredibly self-focused, rarely listening to the adults around them unless a line has been crossed and intervention occurred. They will break through social boundaries because they do not see them, harming themselves unintentionally (running into traffic), harming others (hitting them on the head with a toy) or harming the environment (breaking things).

Rule Oriented (2.0)– Early second-person perspective – Concrete | Collective | Reciprocal

This is the stage that predominates in and is structurally supported by primary schooling.

At around four to six years old, children transition from a first-person (everything is about "me") to a second-person perspective ("we" matters). They mature in this perspective up to, approximately, 10 to 14 years of age. The critical requirement for this reciprocal stage to emerge is when the capacity to visualise develops enough so that the child can step into someone else's shoes and realise that they can "see me in return". Social and emotional development takes a huge leap forward. Reciprocity goes two ways, "If I hurt you, you can hurt me back." Fairness also arises: "one for you and one for me". They now prefer the friend to the toy. Shyness and bashfulness often arise here.

Learning about this new world occurs from trial and error (an inductive experiential process) and the ability to "think" by bringing together their visualisations and talking to themselves. A developing memory of the past allows them to recall in their mind's eye what happened earlier and to hear internally the words of authority figures, providing the capacity to learn from mistakes and not repeat events with undesired consequences. Yet they may forget things because their interior senses of visualisation, inner auditory, and emotions are still developing.

Concrete reasoning also becomes possible when manipulating objects to support the reasoning. The relativity of concrete objects is understood; for example, different shapes have the same area, or two differently shaped cups can hold the same amount of water.

They want to look like and behave like their friends. In their attempt to develop friendships they learn to make agreements about how they will play together and be together. This is the basis of their understanding of rules. They begin to learn that rules keep them safe. Their capacity to prioritise rules is limited, they can easily ascribe the same punishment for a minor offence as a major one.

When they feel cared for by someone they strive to find out what to do to make them happy and whatever feedback they get will stimulate their storage of that action for future use; they interpret every facial expression or interaction to this end. The blunt categorisation of the Egocentric develops a finesse at this stage, based around the gradually increasing rule sets they build to measure the behaviours around them. Those rule sets will come from the most powerful social powers around them, which is often their peers. The shift in perspective from thinking that everyone sees and thinks what they do, to realising that others may be seeing something different means that they are beginning to understand that they may not always know why someone did what they did.

There is an increasing awareness of chronological felt or experienced time. At the Egocentric stage, the sense of time is slippery and confusing. Now they begin to feel a sense of time passing slowly or quickly and can understand hours and half hours; full emergence of time occurs at about 8 years old. With increasing felt time awareness, they can remember the past with greater clarity.

Connection at this stage is to a small group, often a pair or threesome. They look to the person next to them or to the teacher in front; they cannot yet think about everyone. When the group starts to grow it is often an indicator that they are ready to move to the next level.

Conformist (2.5) – Late second-person perspective – Concrete | Collective | Interpenetrative

Children arrive at this stage from as early as 10 years old (and as late as late teens); secondary schools, historically, have structurally supported this stage. Much of the Conformist focus is to make a positive impression and, if need be, to save face – things can only be liked 'ironically', for example. This requires loyalty to the group be it family, peer group or belief system. Symbols, status, appearance, material goods, reputation and prestige assure them that they are fitting into the group.

Tension in relationships is experienced as a threat in that one is either "in" or "out" of a group. Preserving status and approval as a group member is realised by following rules and social norms. Knowing the difference between a major infraction and a minor one reflects an ability to prioritise rules. Individuals begin to establish and internalise principles, observing the reciprocity dynamic to see which patterns are "good" and which are "bad". These principles define the rules of group behaviour, making behaviours more stable and solid, creating an internalised foundation for making choices. There is a commitment to routines, order and stability as a means of safety; traditions are important.

Internalising principles allows a person to persevere in the face of social pressure. These individuals now follow principles and principled people. People that share core principles are "in-group". In-group people will tend to look alike, dress alike, act alike, speak alike and feel alike. They will defend each other. These principles grow to become more important than the spontaneous exchange with peers. Peer pressure begins to recede behind the power and stability of principles.

Conformists can visualise themselves next to someone else, seeing what they see, but cannot yet visualise subtle things they have not seen, so cannot yet project into the future. Mature interior senses make memory reliable, so they can delay gratification and anticipate consequences. They can also reason formally, no longer needing objects to manipulate to figure things out.

Interpenetration with their group supports Conformists to become excessively agreeable and they find it difficult to criticise others, especially those in their immediate circle. They deflect feedback that threatens loss of face and are unable to give individual feedback to others.

Conformists protect the accepted norms and defend the group as well as themselves from any outside influences or attacks that might upset the oneness with the group. They tend not to question authority, and accept group norms, rules, policy and ideas without examination. They keep doing what they do well but feel uncomfortable when they are found wanting in any way, for their primary focus is to interpenetrate with their group. Further, a Conformist will tend to feel that policy, rules and norms prescribe every possible action, and that there is little room for Individual creative risk-taking.

Expert (3.0) – Early third-person perspective – Subtle | Individual | Receptive

The first stage in the Subtle Tier is 3.0 Expert. This stage generally begins in teens or early adulthood when the brain and subtle senses have developed well enough so that they can begin to visualise things they have never seen before. The capacities for outcome, goal, and future orientations – months into the future, even up to two or three years – begin at this stage.

At 1.0 Impulsive, we are cradled concretely in a parent's arms. At 3.0 Expert we are cradled in the arms of respected role models, experts in their field. This comfort provides the safety and trust to develop subtle attachment and subtle bonding. In this new world there is someone there to guide us. This gives us the freedom to be exposed for who we are.

Experts begin to realise that for all the conformity at Conformist, they cannot completely conform. The result is a feeling of a façade, a mask that they wear in public, when deep down inside they are not that which they present themselves to be. This cognitive dissonance resolves by moving into the Expert level and accepting that, despite all attempts at conformity, we are on some level unique human beings. Experts do not abandon their principles but reassess them from the perspective of their unique Individuality. Instead of condemning themselves to a life of guilt over trifles, they now alter some of the principles to allow for, and even celebrate, their uniqueness. The energy that was put into perfecting social conformity now finds a new home in perfecting unique special skills.

As Experts focus more and more on their interior abstract reasoning and developing emotional nuances, they begin to see that these remarkable interiors and emotional capacities define them more than their exterior appearance, recently so prominent for them. Distinctions on the outside such as race, colour and religion are not now as important as the capacities they see on their interior. Inklings that others' interiors are more important than their exteriors also brings human rights and social justice into view. Moreover, they can project themselves into another's shoes and imagine what the other is experiencing beyond what they themselves would experience, if in the same situation.

Abstract reasoning prioritises a focus on details – poring over books – making the Expert far more agile with effectiveness and technical prowess than with efficiency; seeing subtle hierarchies and categories which allow for efficiency may be difficult. They take pride in doing their jobs well and tend to work towards unnecessary perfection while missing deadlines. This supports a tendency to micromanage to ensure things are perfect, often affecting their ability to work well with other people. It is also difficult to prioritise among competing efforts or to grasp the bigger picture. This strong desire to seek improvements and to find perfection plays a vital role in handling the day-to-day running of things.

Experts often develop a belief in the superiority of their own technical abilities and commonly resent criticism, taking it personally; they will dismiss criticism from non-experts, even though they can be quite critical of others and are prone to giving unsolicited advice.

Conformity still has a strong influence on many even though they are pulling away from prior concrete collective expectations. This explains why they are often critical of unfamiliar ways of handling a situation, (relying on established explanations and procedures), but at the same time resent their own expertise being questioned. However, their social focus is more individualistic now. Experts tend to be able to see their own side of a conversation and not the opposing side, commonly giving them the reputation for being argumentative.

Achiever (3.5) – Late third-person perspective – Subtle | Individual | Active

Achievers are readily able to categorise and prioritise the subtle; to see both sides of a situation and make well-reasoned choices. Effectiveness and efficiency are more important than perfection; the 80/20 rule arises. Scientific approaches are an answer to everything. They believe deeply in linear cause and effect and objective rationality. Results are secured by trusting this objective approach, personal conviction, and energy. They can look further forward – five or more years – and have more of a "big picture" orientation

A new quality that has emerged is the capacity to reflect on their thinking and feeling (metacognition). This allows them to see how their thoughts affect their feelings and their feelings affect their thinking, and the resulting insights can change how they behave. The combination of their metacognitive capacities, future orientation, capacity to prioritise and categorise subtle information, ability to see options and make choices, and their active orientation supports their drive to achieve goals and outcomes in the future.

Achievers welcome feedback when it supports reaching their goals. This puts them in a good relationship with people who are working with them and they value teamwork aimed at achieving their goals.

They can project themselves into another's shoes and imagine/predict what they will be experiencing or doing. Attention and focus is on their own individual priorities and thus Achievers live parallel lives with those around them, tending to "talk at" people on subtle levels, rather than "with" them. Balancing different aspects of their life can be difficult.

While Achievers can see other's interiors and goals, they still do not have the natural capacity to see that others are seeing them subtly in return. This sets up subtle competition. Being the best at what they do in comparison to everyone else is valued by Achievers. Just as Egocentrics were unaware of concrete boundaries, Achievers cannot see subtle boundaries. They can crash through others' boundaries, completely unaware of the damage they can do.

Achievers explore their subtle power using the four categories they learned at the Egocentric stage but now in the subtle field. They learn about body language and how to use that to influence people (physical power), they learn about skilled argumentation to advance their goals (intellectual power), they learn how to master their emotions by learning how thoughts affect emotions (emotional power) and they learn social skills of the successful, so they too may be successful (social power). Just like the Egocentric, they can do all these in delightful ways and in intrusive ways.

It is society and culture which sets limits on Achiever intrusiveness; we see culture wars between the Achiever who wants to be free, and the Pluralist Collective that expects politically correct behaviour.

Pluralist (4.0) – Early fourth-person perspective – Subtle | Collective | Reciprocal

Instead of suppressing individual independence in a new collective, the new "rule" is to discover the subtle self without suppression, and this can only be done in reciprocity with others because others can see in you what you cannot see in yourself. Thus, Pluralists become curious about sharing feedback, thoughts, and ideas because they want to know what others are seeing in them.

Vulnerability and courage grow stronger and Pluralists create settings where it is all right to express genuine truths or voices. This open culture allows for more hidden voices to emerge both internally and externally. A person becomes increasingly more tolerant, understanding, respectful and even celebratory about diversity, both internally and externally. All human beings are to be respected, indeed all sentient beings. Those who do not share this belief will be called out and will often be treated without dignity or equality if they persist.

Pluralists realise that their prior sense of objectivity was only a small part of reality; any observer is always sifting what is observed through their own filters. Life is more ambiguous and less predictable than previously imagined; everything is relative to one's context. Focus widens to see assumptions, judgments, ambiguities, and interpretations, though they often cannot yet label them with these words. Pluralists can stand in the contextual shoes of another and see how they and others are socially constructed by their contexts and complex adaptive systems.

Because Pluralists are not yet able to prioritise or categorise contexts, they tend to reduce the hierarchical connections between themselves and others, promoting the importance of two-way reciprocal relationships. Reciprocal approaches to co-creativity can eventually bring about an adaptability in the collective that is unavailable to earlier stages. Goal orientation is no longer prioritised over relationship, and collective processes, often unwieldy, are used for decision-making. Pluralists experience a longer time frame – parent, self, and children's lifetime – 20 or more years forward and back, but oriented to the present.

The core lesson of Pluralist is deep honesty and complete openness, and the result is the discovery of authentic selves and a more open society.

Strategist (4.5) - Late fourth-person perspective – Subtle | Collective | Interpenetrative

This is an Interpenetrative stage, so Strategists take an outside view of systems and contexts and see their intersections, and so have the capacity to construct them as opposed to being socially constructed by them. Strategists can see – and honour – the child and adult developmental trajectory and try to develop behaviours and speech that can be experienced positively by all levels.

The strategist's time frame expands to include three past and three future generations, and their space frame expands to prioritise contexts for the benefit of humanity, the planet, and all living things. Strategists see how they have changed through time and have compassion for the mistakes they made in the past. By having acceptance and compassion for people at all developmental levels, as well as all their current and historical selves, Strategists can make peace with even more of humanity.

Strategists move from simply supporting the sincere expression of each human being and offering dignity for each human condition to creating systems where this dignity becomes a predictable outcome of the system. A hallmark of the Achiever is efficiency, of the Pluralist is depth. Strategists marry these two into efficient systems that support depth of human experience. This provides a great deal of power and wisdom, in helping to shape human systems internally and externally.

Strategists are able to prioritise among competing commitments, opinions and beliefs, tending to value those perspectives that are developmental, people oriented, inclusive of other levels of development, dynamic, and those which foster continuous learning. They can adaptively zoom out with awareness and zoom in with focus. Strategists can co-create and work in collaboration with others to reach outcomes not based on goals but realised by following their ethical principles, which are both subtle and developmental. Understanding when to allow suffering for growth and when to eliminate pointless suffering becomes an important distinction that arises at this developmental level.

Upon reflection, Strategists can identify their own and others' projections onto others. Thus, feedback from all sources is seen as necessary to identify their hidden shadows and to help them grow in self-knowledge and understanding of the world. Strategists value others' perspectives as part of a more complete picture. Strategists can come to a place of deep internal peace, which is not just a temporary relief from intruding thoughts, but something more sustainable. Strategists develop and mature the authentic self as a basic ground of life.

About the author

John Corrigan is the founder of Group 8 Education and works with schools to establish the conditions for twenty-first-century learning. He coaches individuals in how to bring their whole of mind to their day-to-day work, to increase their own effectiveness and that of others. This is his passion.

His 40-year interest in education and learning began as a mathematics undergraduate at Cambridge University, and continued over the years as he gained fluency in several languages.

Leadership experience through multiple careers led to an MBA and work in strategy consulting and corporate planning. While running a professional services firm, John focused on the provision of higher value activities and behaviours to increase the firm's value. He now applies a similar strategy to the education sector to increase value for all stakeholders.

John was born in Manchester and moved to Australia in 1995.

John is the author of five other books:

> *A World Fit for Children* (2005)
> *The Success Zone* (2009) with Andrew Mowat and Doug Long
> *Optimising Time, Attention and Energy (2016)*
> *Red Brain Blue Brain (2019)*
> *Student Feedback (2019)*

Acknowledgements

It takes much more than a single author to create a book of this type that aims to build the case for systemic change in one of society's key institutions.

This book emerged out of one of those moments when many different ideas, thoughts and experiences fall into place and the whole picture comes into focus. The relatively short time in which this happened conceals a lengthy gestation period involving research and conversation with too many educators to count. I thank all of you.

Then the pandemic struck. That gave me the time and additional headspace to turn what I had planned to be a long article into a book. A number of key people made significant contributions. I should like to give special thanks to Jen Haynes, principal of Brisbane Independent School, for generously providing her time, sharing her insights and explaining in detail what she looks for in the teachers she employs – further corroborating my own ideas about what makes an Enlightened teacher. I would also like to thank Terri O'Fallon who developed the STAGES model and introduced me to many of its subtler aspects.

Two other school principals have also contributed greatly through their support and encouragement as my ideas developed. Christina Utri is principal of CRC St Albans and kept me grounded whilst encouraging me to reach higher. Gerald Bain-King, formerly of CBC St Kilda, very generously provided his time and advice as the book developed, using his experiences in creating art to point me towards ways to stimulate my own thinking. I cannot thank him enough for this help and for his story in the book.

To the two students, 'Jackson' and 'Alexander', it was a pleasure to speak with you both and share your experiences in school. I have no doubt that both of you will do great things in life.

I am most grateful to my editor Nicola Dunnicliff-Wells for her advice and suggestions which have, once again, made this a much better book.

To my wife Maryse for your support during our shared lockdown in Melbourne, thank you.

Lightning Source UK Ltd.
Milton Keynes UK
UKHW020641100820
367987UK00018B/1869